WATT'S M

WATT'S
MY NAME

An Autobiography

JIM WATT

with Norman Giller

STANLEY PAUL

London Melbourne Sydney Auckland Johannesburg

Stanley Paul & Co. Ltd

An imprint of the Hutchinson Publishing Group

3 Fitzroy Square, London W1P 6JD

Hutchinson Group (Australia) Pty Ltd
30–32 Cremorne Street, Richmond South, Victoria 3121
PO Box 151, Broadway, New South Wales 2007

Hutchinson Group (NZ) Ltd
32–34 View Road, PO Box 40-086, Glenfield, Auckland 10

Hutchinson Group (SA) (Pty) Ltd
PO Box 337, Bergvlei 2012, South Africa

First published 1981

© Jim Watt and Norman Giller 1981

Set in VIP Baskerville by
A-Line Services, Saffron Walden, Essex

Printed in Great Britain by The Anchor Press Ltd,
and bound by Wm Brendon & Son Ltd,
both of Tiptree, Essex

ISBN 0 09 145380 1

Contents

To
the memory of Joyce
and to
Mum for having me,
Margaret for loving me,
Sylvie for spoiling me,
Terry for managing me,
And all my ain folk o' Scotland

I couldn't have done it without
your support.

Scots, wha hae wi' Wallace bled,
Scots wham Bruce has aften led,
Welcome to your gory bed,
Or to victorie.
                    Robert Burns (1759–96)

'Box with your brains as well
as your fists.'
                    Tommy Burns (1881–1955)

Acknowledgements

Copyright photographs are acknowledged as follows: *Daily Star*; *Evening Times*; *Glasgow Herald*; Terry Kirk; *Scottish Daily Record*; Sportapics

Seconds Out

A man finds out about himself in the boxing ring. Questions are asked and you have to dig deep for the answers. There can be no lying or deceiving. You get the naked truth about your courage, the extent of your commitment and the depth of your stamina and endurance. Like no other sport, boxing separates the men from the boys.

I found out about myself the night I defended my world lightweight championship against Sean O'Grady. The question I was forced to ask myself in the ninth round as blood pumped from a gash by my right eye was: 'How badly do you want to keep your title?' My answer was to reach down into untapped mental reserves and discover a willpower that lifted me to victory when everything looked lost. That night, I proved myself the man while O'Grady was the boy.

He was cut on his forehead after our heads had collided in the tenth round and suddenly it was *his* turn to have to answer the question of how desperately he wanted the title. For O'Grady, the answer was a negative one. He could not match my desire to win and from the moment the kid from Oklahoma was cut he was a beaten fighter. Boxing is as much a psychological as physical sport and my mind was proved stronger than O'Grady's after our flesh had been exposed as equal. As my manager, Terry Lawless, wiped the blood from my face seconds after the fight had been stopped in the twelfth round, I said: 'This will make a great chapter for the book . . .!'

I give a full breakdown on the fight with O'Grady later in this book, but before you get there I invite you to share my memories of the tears and the triumphs, the laughter and the falls that I've had on my way to the top of the mountain.

This is not just a book about boxing. It is about life and, sadly, death; about a city and its people, a country and its pride. It is a modern fairy story with real flesh and blood characters. I should know because much of the blood spilt is mine.

I am anxious not to bore anybody with a blow-by-blow account of my ring career. There is a complete summary of my fighting record in the Scrapbook at the back which gives the media version of how I became a modern Cinderella Man of the ring and stayed around to have a real ball.

As I prepare the book, my sport is under severe attack from the abolitionists. The tragic death of that brave lion of Wales, Johnny Owen, after a world title fight in Los Angeles has, not for the first time, brought boxing under the microscope of people who can neither stand nor *under*stand the sport. We all weep for Johnny. But to ban boxing would in my opinion do more harm than good to dozens of young men who find the ring a place for self-expression and personal fulfilment. The risks and the rewards can be great, but nobody puts a gun to a boxer's head and forces him to climb through the ropes.

Boxing has given me an escape route from what could so easily have been a life of drudgery and dole queues. I want to see that escape route remain open so that the young Johnny Owens and Jim Watts of this world can have the opportunity to make something of themselves.

This book is all about how boxing helped shape me into the man that I am. I've *talked* my story and I would like to thank writer Norman Giller for getting my words down onto paper in some sort of order. Our objective has been to keep it all on a conversational level and we hope you are entertained on the following pages, particularly by some of the humour that is an important part of the world in which I live.

Oh, by the way: Jim Watt's my name.

Jim Watt

I Belong to Glasgow

The story I have to tell is of two Jim Watts. There is the Jim Watt I used to be in the days when I had to suffer the taunts of being called Jim Who. Then there is the Jim Watt I am now, a world boxing champion nearing the close of my career with a treasure chest of memories that will warm me when the fighting is over and the only bells I answer are on alarm clocks.

To start at the beginning: I answered the first bell of life on 18 July 1948. My mother, Ina, tells me it was a Sunday and she should know because she was there at the time. Her first words to the midwife working in our corner were, 'He's got a face like a wee boxer.' She's some woman, my Mum. It is only now after experience as a parent that I realize and appreciate just how special she has been in my life. Even Terry Lawless would have to give ground to her as the Manager of the Century.

For the first couple of years of my life, I lived with my Mum, Dad and elder sister, Jean, in a single-room apartment in Bridgeton on Glasgow's east side. Writer Hugh McIlvanney, that gifted Scottish observer of the sports scene, describes the area as 'the sort of place Jaws would swim through in a hurry in case he was molested.'

We then moved to a rented room-and-kitchen apartment in a tenement block in Possilpark at the north end of Glasgow. Jaws would have been well advised to give that area a miss, too. There are some razor-sharp people around the place who would have quickly been selling him off in soup tins.

I have just two memories of my Dad. He worked in a bakery and I can recall rushing down the street on thin, four-year-old legs to meet him and collect my daily present of a cream cake or bun. The other memory is a painful one. It is of him lying in bed in the corner of our room coughing. Always coughing. He died of chronic bronchitis. He was thirty-eight and I was barely five.

Being without a father helped shape me into the person and the champion that I became. I learnt very early in life to be independent and stand on my own two feet. In the inevitable primary school playground scraps most boys were able to threaten you with their fathers and brothers. I had nobody to fight my battles for me. I didn't know my father well enough to miss him and grew up as 'the man of the house'.

I have not got a sob story to tell about living on poverty street. My mother was such an industrious woman and such a good manager that I was never aware of having less than anybody else in Possilpark where you could count the millionaires on the fingers of Venus de Milo. One of the most important factors in my make-up is my pride. I am fiercely proud of being Scottish, of being a Glaswegian, of being a world champion. Proud of everything in which I am involved. It is only now that I analyse myself for this book that I realize I inherited this proudness from my mother. She always made my sister Jean and me take pride in our appearance and taught us good manners and right from wrong. 'I want to be proud of you,' she used to say. That was an important word in the vocabulary of the Watt household. *Proud*.

My mother was proud to the point of bloody-mindedness. Because she was a widow, Jean and I were entitled to have free dinners at school, but Mum wouldn't hear of it. 'We don't want charity,' she used to insist and always scraped together enough money to enable us to pay for our school meals each week. She used to slog away in a hospital laundry for £7 a week. It should have been ten times that for the risks she took with her health. She was always having to receive inoculations because of the dangers of contamination from the hospital gear that she used to wash. I think my Mum's had nearly as many jabs in her arm as I've had jabs on the nose.

Because Mum was out working all hours, my sister Jean had to carry a lot of responsibility and was like a second mother to me. We didn't fight like other brothers and sisters;

we grew up the best of friends, which is the way it has remained. Mind you, if Jean had her way she would not let me lace on another boxing glove. She has always hated the thought of me fighting.

I was so independent as a youngster that I had the key of the door at the age of six. It was tied to a long piece of string that was looped around my neck so that I could let myself into the apartment when Mum was at the laundry.

I've got a story to tell about my Mum that is right out of a kid's comic. When I was about ten I was aware that most of the kids down our street had a bike; maybe one that had to be shared with brothers and sisters but nevertheless they had a bike. When you're ten and aching to possess something, you don't stop to consider economics. So I asked my Mum if I could have a bike. To her on a weekly wage of just £7, it must have sounded as if I was asking her to clear the national debt. 'Och, they're dangerous things,' she said dismissively. That, I thought, was the end of the subject. But my mother's pride was at work. A few weeks later, the bike forgotten, she asked me to go to the shops with her to help carry the bags. As I walked past the bicycle shop I cast an envious eye in the window and was astonished to see my mother suddenly stop and walk into the showroom. Ten minutes later, after the payment of a deposit and the signing of hire-purchase forms, I emerged wheeling a gleaming new bike. For the next twelve months I rode down to the shop once a week to pay the ten-bob instalments.

As many Glaswegians will be able to tell you, the advantage of starting with nothing in life is that everything comes as a bonus. That bicycle was my first big bonus. But the main bonus of which I am now gratefully aware is of having had a Mum in a million.

It is only now as I look back on my life that I realize just how much I owe to boxing. I grew up in an environment that bred violence, but thanks to boxing I didn't get caught up in the Glasgow ghetto gang wars that left several of my Possilpark acquaintances with scars for life. The frightening razor wars of the 1960s held no attraction for me. It has never been in my nature to be violent outside the ring, but if it had not been for the demands of my boxing career, I might have gone running wild with some of my more boisterous pals. They were searching for an identity and found an outlet for their aggression as members of gangs who had a common bond of hating authority. Unlike the bully-boy football hooligans you get today, they did not pick on innocent people, but only on rival gang members.

Thankfully, I found my identity through boxing. Otherwise I might well have ended up working as a nine-to-five electrician if and when jobs were available. I had brief experience of being on the dole between fights in the early stages of my career and my heart bleeds over the humiliation all the unemployed people have to suffer when they collect their social security money. It angers me to hear know-nothing critics lucky to be in work dismissing the unemployed as spongers and layabouts. Of course there are liberty-takers, but most redundant Scots are victims of the recession. I have stood in the queues with them waiting to be paid out and have been touched almost to tears by the depth of their despair and feeling of hopelessness.

Boxing is a great sport for giving no-hopers the chance to make something of themselves and to get a start in life that would be denied them without the cash they earn with their fists.

The combination of being born and raised in Glasgow and becoming a boxer helped make me the man I am and you won't find me knocking my sport or my city. I get irritated when I hear Glasgow being painted as a dungeon of a city. Those heard to say that it is their least favourite city don't really know the place or its people.

Glasgow has many faces and many facets. Most Glaswegians are warm, generous people and in the rough, working-class area where I grew up there may have been a lack of money but never a lack of comradeship and certainly no lack of pride. The homes might have been sparsely furnished, but they were kept spotlessly clean and there was always a welcome in them for any visitors.

I can't make out a case for Glasgow being the prettiest of

cities, but if you care to take a walk on a bright sunlit day along the riverside in the region of Victoria Bridge at Strathclyde I think you will find Glasgow able to stand comparison with many of the more reputedly elegant cities.

You will find all human life in Glasgow. The demon drink, of course, plays a part in orchestrating the lives of many of the city's inhabitants. If you are in the city at night when the pubs are turning out you can see sights that are at the same time both hilarious and horrifying. There is nothing quite so funny as watching a drunk staggering along on legs that are totally out of control. There is also nothing quite so sad because many of the drunks have turned to the bottle as an escape from reality. On the other hand there are many perfectly sober Glaswegians who drink only in moderation and who share my love for a city that is always throbbing with life and laughter. There is an undercurrent of tension in the poor quarters of Glasgow where the recession bites hardest, yet these are the places where the laughter is loudest.

Glasgow humour is about as subtle as a barbed-wire fence. We tend to use our humour as a defensive weapon and if you wander the streets of our city you will come across legions of budding Billy Connollys drawing laughs from everyday life and events. I have a reputation as being something of a joker outside the ring, but I usually get my laughs at somebody else's expense, never intending to hurt, but just using people as unsuspecting stooges for my punch-lines. It is typical, brutal Glaswegian humour and somehow reflects the city in which I was born and bred.

We like to laugh at real stories that have a touch of aggression to them, like when an acquaintance of mine was recently sitting at red traffic lights in Gallowgate. The car in front had a sticker in the back window that read, 'If you love Jesus sound your horn.' A little sheepishly, my friend made a public declaration of his love for Jesus by beeping his horn. The driver's door of the car in front swung open and my friend was suddenly confronted by a large and angry motorist shaking his fist down at him. 'Ah'll gie ye the heid, Jimmy,' he threatened. 'Canny ye see the lights are still red. . . ?'

I am a proud son of Glasgow and representing the city and

my country in the ring is one of my greatest motivations. I shall always be thankful for the support I have received from my ain folk and the world lightweight title belongs as much to Glasgow and to Scotland as to me.

The one side of Glasgow life that sometimes appals me is the religious rivalry that occasionally comes to the surface with a poisonous venom. I am a God-fearing person and follow my faith privately in my head and my heart. I always pray before fights but never for victory, only that I get into the ring in good health and with full fitness and that I leave it without injury. This reminds me of the priest who was sitting ringside watching a boxing tournament. One of the contestants crossed himself just before the bell rang and a spectator asked the priest: 'What does that mean?' 'Nothing, if he can't fight,' the priest replied.

I am a Protestant and before my world title defence against Irish Catholic Charlie Nash a reporter, hoping for some sort of sensational response, asked me if I was in any way prejudiced.

'Oh yes,' I said. 'My wife is a Catholic. My manager is a Catholic with Irish ancestry. Frank Black, who helps with my training, is an Irish Catholic. Mickey Duff, the promoter of the fight and a good friend, is the Polish-born son of a rabbi and my best pal among the others boxers is Maurice Hope, a black Catholic who was born in the West Indies.

'Yes, I'm prejudiced. I'm prejudiced against prejudice.'

The very first punch that I can remember throwing bloodied my opponent's nose and disrupted a football match. I was eleven at the time. It happened while I was a touchline spectator at a junior match in a public park. The linesman, a hefty boy who was a couple of years older than me, insisted that all spectators took a couple of paces back so that he could run the line properly. Everybody shuffled back to order. Everybody except me. I took only one pace back because I was smaller than the people around me and couldn't see the action. The linesman had run out of patience and shoved me in the chest to remove me from his path. Jim Watt came back fighting. I rushed at him and caught him a swinging right-hand punch bang on the nose. The things I remember most about the incident were the sight of blood suddenly spurting across his face and the fact that he was holding a flag in one hand and an apple in the other. Now I had *my* hands full as he came back with a counterattack and I was getting much the better of the exchanges when we were pulled apart by players and the referee. The game was held up while the trainer mopped the blood off the linesman's face. The referee insisted that we shake hands before he would wave play on.

For the first time in my life I then experienced the *fear* of fighting. While the game was still in progress my mates gleefully fed me stories about the linesman's ability with his fists. Apparently he was a local junior boxing champion and the clear view of the people surrounding me was that I was going to get the hiding of my life once the match was over. There was no way I would have agreed to a return clause! I wanted to disappear quietly, but my pride wouldn't let me. For the next twenty minutes or so my stomach churned and my legs turned to jelly. I wasn't scared of getting hurt, but of being made to look a fool in front of my mates.

When the final whistle went, the linesman left a cluster of players – he was a reserve for one of the teams – and came towards me with a tin of biscuits in his hand. I braced myself ready for defensive action and almost collapsed with relief when he held out the tin and offered me a biscuit. It was his peace offering and clearly he shared my fears about a return fight.

This *fear* of fighting has remained with me to this day. I have, of course, got the fear under control, but it is there nonetheless. My stomach still churns when I think ahead to a fight. I have never had a fear of taking punches, but I worry about letting people down. My family, my manager, my friends and supporters. Myself. Believe me, the worrying is harder than the actual fighting. I am a born worrier rather than a born warrior.

But I know that I *need* the fear. I feed off it and it helps motivate me. That great Olympic hero Jesse Owens used to say that if he didn't feel nervous when he went to his blocks, he knew he would not be able to perform at his peak. It is the same with me. I even go so far as manufacturing pressures for myself to make sure I have got the right amount of nervous tension for a fight. The day I don't feel fear about fighting is the day I'll quit boxing.

Once I even spent £72,000 that I didn't have to put pressure on myself going into a vital fight to add that extra impetus and desire to win. But I'll tell you about that later in the book. Meantime, back to the story of the Jim Watt I used to be. . . .

I came into boxing by accident. At school my sporting dreams were of being another Jim Baxter or Pat Crerand, paralysing England with a procession of passes from midfield. I was more of a Walter Mitty than a Walter McGowan. In the year below me at school, there was another wee laddie dreaming of a footballing future. He turned his dreams into reality. His name was Kenny Dalglish.

If you had asked me the top twenty things I wanted to do with my life, boxing would not have got into the list. It was a sport as foreign to me as baseball or show jumping (there are not too many equestrian centres in Possilpark where a fence is somebody who handles hot property; a clear round is when everybody drains their glasses and waits for the refills).

I have to thank the weatherman for my boxing career. I was a promising parks footballer but was frozen out of the game in the winter of 1963. Thick snow made all the pitches unplayable and I was at a loose end as to what to do with my spare time. I saw a poster inviting boys to come and learn the Noble Art at the Cardowan Amateur Boxing Club at George's Cross, Maryhill. Having tried judo without it getting a hold on me, I decided I might as well have a bash at boxing and went along to the gymnasium with Joe Glencross, whose cousin Tommy later became British featherweight champion. The gym was closed. Joe and I were about to shrug it off as a wasted journey when we were spotted by Andy Munro, a keen supporter of the club, who just happened to be passing. 'The gym isn't open tonight,' he told us. 'Come back the same time tomorrow evening and Jim Murray will be delighted to see you.'

If Andy had not met us I doubt if I would have been sufficiently interested to return to the gymnasium and my career would never have got off the ground. Some eighteen years later Andy remains a good pal of mine; he works with me in my garage business and is always around to encourage me when I'm training on my own in Glasgow.

Jim Murray. It was the first time I had heard of the man who was to play such an influential part in my life over the next thirteen years. I have a lot to thank him for and my gratitude far outweighs my annoyance over some aggravating incidents towards the end of our association. Murray is something of an eccentric with very strong ideals and principles. He is a middle-aged bachelor who is totally dedicated to boxing, physical fitness and healthy living. Apart from boxing, he also teaches Yoga and is a health-food nut. He has deep left-wing political views and can quote from speeches by his idol, Nye Bevan. His influence over me went beyond the usual boxer–trainer relationship and he became like a Svengali figure in my life, reaching the point where he used to advise me what to eat, drink and read. I recall that he was heavily into Raymond Chandler as an author and fed me a hefty diet of Philip Marlowe stories.

He could slip into infuriating moods of stubbornness when things were not running for him but nobody could ever dispute that he really cared about the welfare of his boxers and he would go to great lengths to see that they were fairly matched. No Cardowan boxer was ever put into the ring out of his depth. I recall Murray once leading one of my clubmates into the ring for an amateur contest and removing his dressing-gown ready for the introductions. He then looked at the opposite corner and realized the opponent was not the one he had agreed to. The opponent was from the right club and even the right family, but was an elder and heavier brother. Quietly and without fuss, Murray slipped the gown back on to his boxer and led him back to the dressing-room without a punch being thrown. There were many cornermen who would not have noticed that a ringer had been slipped in as opposition and, sadly, not all of them would have cared.

The first time Jim Murray saw me shape up with gloves on,

he growled at me for going into a southpaw stance, which for the unitiated means I led with my right fist and right foot forward. He persuaded me to switch to an orthodox stance and encouraged me to persevere when I said that I felt awkward. I could get my fists working all right but my legs just wouldn't obey me. I was stumbling around like Long John Silver with woodworm and Murray finally agreed that the southpaw style was right for me. That was the best break I ever had. I know I would not have made the grade with an orthodox stance. It is no coincidence that Britain's three most recent world champions (Alan Minter, Maurice Hope and myself) are all southpaws. We are awkward cusses to fight. For our opponents, it is like having to drive on the wrong side of the road when they meet us in the ring. I am right-handed and it is my strongest fist, so I lead with my heaviest punches whereas most boxers leading with the left are jabbing with the weaker hand and use their stronger fist, the right, only sparingly.

I quit boxing twice during the first couple of months of training. The reason was a simple one. I didn't like getting punched on the nose. The first time it happened in a sparring session, tears came to my eyes and I thought that I would stick to football. I missed the following training session and Murray came to my home to encourage me to return to the gym. He had spotted something in my make-up that convinced him I had what it takes to get to the top.

He went out of his way again a few weeks later to coax me back into training after I had taken another couple of punches that killed my appetite for the sport. I will be eternally grateful to him for pumping me up with the confidence to continue boxing.

In January 1964 I had my first amateur contest and won inside two minutes. My career was off the launching pad.

But to this day I still don't like taking a punch on the nose and under Jim Murray I developed a defensive style of boxing that was possibly too negative, but saved me from taking any unnecessary punishment.

Jim and I went as far as we possibly could together. We broke up mainly because of our failure to attract the major promoters. I have to share the blame because I was too negative in the ring and promoters wanted me for their commercial shows like they wanted pneumonia. I boxed on only one top-line London bill and had sixteen of my twenty-nine fights under Murray's management on private club shows. On the plus side, I won the British championship and challenged for the Commonwealth title, but the money I was earning would have been like pocket money for other champions I could name. It was because I boxed so often behind closed doors that I was tagged Jim Who. The general boxing public just didn't know me from Adam. Or Eve, for that matter.

Jim Murray and I parted on less than amicable terms after I had been robbed of a points victory in a European title eliminator against Frenchman André Holyk in Lyons in October 1975. I decided that he could do no more to motivate me and my plan was to manage myself and earn some quick money before getting out of a sport which no longer had any appeal for me. Then I made a telephone call that was to change my whole life.

Round 2

The Call That Changed
My Life

It was the winter of 1976 and the Jim Watt I used to be was planning two or three more fights before retirement when there was a message left at my home in Moodiesburn: 'Telephone Terry Lawless.'

This is how I recall our telephone conversation one late January evening:

'It's Jim Watt here, Terry. I got your message to call you.'

'I bet I'm the first manager you've had to call long-distance. That's not good business for a canny Scot. Now before this conversation goes any further, have you got a manager?'

'No, Terry. I've split with Jim Murray. We have gone as far as we could together. I've had a few managers chasing me, but they've not come up with anything that interests me. The way I see it, I'm going to have a couple or maybe three more fights to get some money in the bank and then call it a day.'

'That doesn't sound very progressive thinking for a British champion.'

'Look, I'm twenty-seven. I'm not thinking about progress as much as profit. I'm not getting anywhere with my career. The only ambition I've left is to win a Lonsdale Belt outright and then retire. I've got a motor business and I want to concentrate full time on that – once I've banked some money from my last few fights.'

'I'm sorry to hear you adopting this defeatist attitude, Jim. I don't think you've really reached your full potential. Jim Murray's done a really good job with you in the circumstances. I know how difficult it must be to get work up there in

Scotland. I'd like to help you get the exposure you deserve – to my mind you're the best lightweight in Europe.'

'I'm flattered by your interest, Terry, but I'm going to need time to think things over before committing myself to anything.'

'Take as long as you like. There's no rush. I've been following your career ever since you knocked out my star fighter John Stracey in the ABA semifinals. You've got all the time in the world on your side. You don't need me or anybody to manage you if you mean it about having only two or three more fights. But I've got a long-term programme I'd like to put to you if you do happen to change your mind. . . .'

When I put the telephone down I was aware of that tingling sensation you get when something big is about to happen in your life. I recalled the first time I had been aware of Terry Lawless's presence in a dressing-room. I was getting gloved up for a fight in Nottingham where he was matchmaker. He had come into the dressing-room to see how things were progressing and within a minute of joining us the place was alive with laughter. It lifted the usual morgue-like atmosphere and I thought then what a good bloke he was to have in your company.

His sense of humour appealed to me and I knew there was no better manager in Britain, possibly the world. He had guided so many boxers to British and European titles that he was known as the Champion Maker. Just ten weeks earlier he had steered John Stracey to a stunning world welterweight championship victory over the great José Napoles in Mexico. Stracey, the fighter I had knocked out in forty-five seconds, was on top of the world while I felt at the bottom of mine.

I thought long and hard before agreeing to meet Terry for further talks. At that winding-down stage in my career I knew I could not afford a single mistake. There would be no going back and I didn't want to let either myself or Terry down by making a wrong decision. I discussed Terry's approach with my wife Margaret and my business partner Arthur Morrison because I knew that if I joined him it would mean training in London which would be an inconvenience to both of them. Yet in my heart I already knew that I would agree to join the

27

Lawless camp. He had re-awakened the competitor in me and I sensed that telephone call would prove a good investment.

A week later we met each other halfway in Birmingham. I travelled down with a good pal of mine, Eddie Coakley, and told him to leave us alone for a few hours while we talked business. When Eddie rejoined us four hours later, Terry and I had not yet got around to talking about basic boxing matters. It was the first real conversation that we'd had together and we struck up an instant rapport. For four hours we discussed everything under the sun and it was only when Eddie reappeared that we realized that the time had passed so quickly. It sounds maybe corny to say it, but we had got along as if we had known each other for years. Friendship at first sight, Terry called it.

We found we were on the same wavelength on so many things outside boxing, such as a similar taste in music, books, humour, television shows and personalities. When we finally got down to talking about boxing, he took my breath away by discussing a three-year plan. He mapped out a programme in which I would have four or five quick fights to build up a public and a following outside Scotland and then a stepping stone of title fights in which, if everything went smoothly, I would win a Lonsdale Belt outright, take the European championship and then possibly get a big pay day by fighting for the world crown. If it had been anybody else but Terry Lawless saying that I would have considered him a nut case. But this was a man so respected in boxing that I had to go along with his thinking even though deep down I was only really interested in getting one big-money purse. We shook hands and from that day on I was a Terry Lawless fighter.

I quickly discovered that Terry is more than just a manager to his fighters. He is like a father to them, a caring, conscientious man who is the total opposite to the popular image of boxing managers.

I have fallen out with him only once since joining his East London camp. And that was over money. The fact that he refused to take any from me! For my first five fights under his management he gave me all my purse in full without stopping his 25 per cent commission. He said the reason was he had not been able to get me the pay days I deserved and that he would take his cut when we hit the jackpot. His confidence in me was remarkable. I found it embarrassing and almost had to have an argument with him before he would agree to take his share. He finally and reluctantly accepted my point that his charitable action was boosting my bank balance but damaging my conscience. I desperately wanted him to be rewarded for everything he was doing to breath boxing life back into my body and mind.

There is no way that I can repay Terry and his family for all that they have done for me. His wife Sylvie treats me like a son when I stay at their Romford home before fights. When I was a young fighter just starting out in the game, my mother and my sister Jean used to turn their schedule upside down to suit me. Meals were cooked to fit in with my training and I was given every care and consideration to make sure my preparations were helped and never hindered. That is how it is for me when I am at the Lawless household. Nothing is too much trouble for Sylvie, who won't even hoover upstairs during the day when I am sleeping off a hard training session.

Sylvie is as much Terry's partner as his wife and is as knowledgeable about boxing business as many people in the game. Their teenage son, Stephen, is a fifth-form schoolboy and another Terry Lawless in the making. Like his father, he loves the history of the sport and keeps records of all the world's major fights and fighters. It would have been understandable if he had been jealous of all the attention I receive when I virtually take over the Lawless home but he is one of my biggest supporters and I value his friendship. Their married daughter, Lorraine, is her dad's number one fan and none of his boxers can do any wrong in her eyes.

Terry admits he would not be half the person he is without the strength and love of his family around him. And that is also how it is for me.

A Family Man

Every punch that I throw and the few that I take are all in a good cause. The more money I can make, the more secure the future will be for my family who matter most of all to me. My wife, Margaret, my sons, Andrew and Jim Junior, and my darling daughter, Michelle, are really what Jim Watt is all about. They have given me the will and the reason to fight like hell to stay on top in a profession where both the risks and the rewards can be great.

Margaret has been of enormous strength to me and copes with my pre-fight moods that would put a strain on many marriages. She protects me from pressures at home and takes all the household decisions that I should at least share. I wonder if she knew what she was letting herself in for when she married me? We met at the Barrowland dance hall in Glasgow (I've been leading her a dance ever since) and I didn't tell her I was a fighter. She was a machinist at the time and I told her I was an electrician, which I was because never in my career have I been a full-time boxer. One of her friends told her I was a fighter and she wouldn't believe it until I took her home and showed her some of the trophies I had won. Thanks to having been able to slip out of the way of most of the punches thrown at me, I have few tell-tale trade marks and have (touch wood) managed to avoid the traditional flattened nose.

I can tell a deeply sad story that illustrates the way Margaret has helped me to put my career first ahead of the normal considerations a wife is entitled to expect from her husband. It is a story that will also reveal that boxers are not the animals they are made out to be. Take it from me, boxers are human beings with feelings like everyone else. When we are preparing for a fight we have to try to shut out all outside pressures and problems. This was particularly so for my world title defence against Howard Davis, the most important fight of my life.

Just six weeks before the contest we were hit by a shattering tragedy that completely broke down my walls of single-minded concentration. My lovely sister-in-law, Joyce, dropped dead. We had no warning. It was as sudden as a light going out. She was just a week off her twenty-first birthday, a caring mother of three bonny children aged from one month to three years.

She and Margaret were not just sisters. They were best friends. All their lives they had shared everything and were as close as any two people I know. For my Margaret, it was as if part of her world had been chopped away. The pain for her was (and is) more severe than words can describe.

The memory of the day Joyce died burns in my mind like a red-hot poker. We had planned for it to be such a happy day.

For weeks I had been looking around for a good second-hand family car for her and her husband, Willie. I found it in time for it to be a twenty-first birthday present for Joyce and when Willie came to my garage sales showroom to collect it he was as pleased as a boy collecting a new toy. As he drove off home to show the car to Joyce, I left the garage to go to the gymnasium to train.

I was just doing my early exercises after changing into my boxing kit, when my business partner Arthur Morrison called me. He said that Margaret had phoned the garage but was too hysterical to make any sense. I immediately thought that something had happened to one of our three children and dashed across Glasgow to my Moodiesburn home, a fear-driven car journey of which I have little recollection.

When I arrived home I learned the terrible truth. Willie had told Joyce he would beep the horn when he got back with the car so that she could show it to the children. He beeped once, twice, three times, but without any response. When he finally went inside the house to call Joyce, he found her lying on their bed, dead from a brain haemorrhage.

I recall this terrible day not for reasons of sensation but to reveal the cloud of misery that dropped over my family and me with the most challenging contest of my career just weeks away. I was just coming into the most vital part of my training schedule, the month that I spend before every fight with Terry Lawless in London. And it was the time when my Margaret needed me most of all. I agonized over what to do. Everybody was sympathetic, particularly promoters Mickey Duff and Mike Barrett. Nobody put any pressure on me. As Terry said to me: 'There is nothing anybody can say or advise at a time like this. We will go along with anything you want to do. The decision has to be yours and yours alone.'

In the end, though, I opted out and let Margaret make the decision for me. 'You've got to go to London as planned,' she said. 'You must prepare properly for this fight.'

Margaret knew what the fight meant to me, and to us as a family, and did not wish to burden herself with the blame if anything went wrong. It turned out to be the best thing for her when I left for London because she had to force herself into a routine that made her grief just about manageable.

There was no way I could have called for a postponement of the fight. Ibrox Park would have been lost for the promotion because of the approaching football season. There was the threat that I could have been stripped of the title for refusing to go through with a defence at the agreed date and venue. A world-wide TV deal would have been wrecked and there was the possibility of Scotland losing the fight to the United States, which would have robbed me of the vital backing of my ain folk. So I left Margaret alone with her grief and slipped away to London with only the Howard Davis fight in my mind. Everything else was blocked out.

As a professional, I know what I did was right. But it was a devastating experience that forced me to question my priorities and it made me fully appreciate the importance in my life of Margaret and my family.

All I know is that to climb to the top where I am and then stay there you have to be totally single-minded. In world championship boxing you must have complete dedication to survive. But we do have feelings. Deep, deep feelings.

32

For me, family life is all important. Margaret and the children come first in all my non-boxing considerations. My home is my sanctuary and when I'm away from the ring that's where I like to be best with the people I love most. Once I have got a fight over and done with, I have little to do with the boxing scene. I have a full life away from the game and most of the friends we mix with on the social side have nothing to do with boxing. Three Glasgow sportswriters, John Quinn, Jim Reynolds and Dick Currie, are regular companions away from their world of deadlines and headlines, and our close-knit circle of friends includes my partner Arthur Morrison and his wife Christine, Harriet and Bernie Griffin, who are towers of strength to Margaret when I'm away training, Eddie Coakley and, the one boxing man, Walter McGowan, who knows when not to talk shop and has a sense of humour that would liven up any company.

I make no apologies if this is beginning to read like a Jimmy Young record-request slot. The people I have mentioned are important to me and have all played their part in helping Margaret and me through the difficult times on the way to the world championship.

Margaret insists on watching all my fights although she gets sick with nerves every time I climb into the ring. She doesn't mention it, but I am sure that as far as she is concerned my retirement cannot come soon enough. I would like to step off the mountain at the top as undefeated champion, but the hardest thing for any sportsman is to know when to retire. I have taken a long time fighting my way to the top and it demands enormous discipline to get out while the pickings are at their richest. I feel like a hard-working farmer who after many almost barren seasons has suddenly landed a bumper harvest. It is difficult not to hang around eating the fruit.

But as I prepare this book I am thinking of just one or perhaps two more defences of my title. I shall then concentrate on my motor businesses, possibly get involved in boxing promotions in Scotland and, hopefully, do some radio and TV commentating work which I enjoy very much.

The big danger, of course, is that I shall hang around like a late-stop guest at a party and have one drink too many. One

33

fight too many is something I must be careful to avoid. Muhammad Ali is a sad and telling example of somebody who went to the well once too often and found that it had suddenly dried up.

I enjoy the feeling of being a world champion, although, to be honest, winning the title has been one big anticlimax. So much mental and physical energy goes into my build-up for fights, that it's a big let-down when they are all over. Celebrations always fall flat for me because I am suddenly exhausted from the extreme concentration. It burns me out and I feel empty for at least two days after each contest. All I can say from my experiences is that the winning is not so good as the losing is bad. Defeat is a monster that eats me up inside and I would rather have not competed than lose.

Sometimes I wonder if I will ever be content with anything that I do. I am my own worst critic and rarely feel satisfied with what I achieve. Perfectionism is a disease from which I suffer and unless I can do something extremely well I don't want to know about it. My hobby is playing finger-picking blues guitar. I have reached a fair standard, but because I want to be the best at anything I do, I'm not very happy with my playing. I would like to reach John Williams's standards, but tend to play more like Esther Williams, with webbed fingers! I love playing golf yet torture myself with self-criticism if I am not getting down in par, which is often.

The BBC telephoned me before one of my world title fights and asked me if I would like to play around with Alice. I said I would love to but that my wife wouldn't be too pleased. What they meant, of course, was a round with Peter Alliss, who is my idea of what a golfer and a commentator should be: suave, sophisticated, stylish, and with a dream of a swing and a delivery line at the microphone that is always entertaining as well as informative.

I like to see people with real style in sport and this is what I am always striving to achieve for myself. I don't want just to be a world champion. I want to *look* good while I'm about it.

This continual search for perfection means I can sometimes be a swine to live with and I am full of admiration and appreciation for the way Margaret handles my moods. I don't

34

think anybody quite realizes the stress my winning the title has thrown on to her. She is suddenly having to cope with living in a goldfish bowl. The day I won the world title our private lives virtually went out the window. We can't move in Glasgow without somebody stopping us to talk, ask for autographs and generally inquire after my health. It's all very nice and flattering and the time to worry is when they stop showing an interest, but it can also be enormously demanding on your time and attempts at privacy.

It builds to a peak in the month leading up to a fight and Margaret is left to handle the explosion of interest on her own because I'm away down to London for my training. It's the price of fame and I marvel at the way Margaret manages to contend with it all and still run a house and look after our three lively kids.

The pressure even reaches down and touches our children. Our ten-year-old son, Andrew, is the target for a lot of ribbing at school because all the publicity I get, but he takes it in his stride provided I'm winning! Michelle, our three-year-old daughter, is already so accustomed to grabbing the attention of visiting photographers and reporters that she gets quite haughty if they don't take notice of her. Margaret was so engrossed in an interview with a woman's magazine reporter once that Michelle felt she was being ignored and decided to draw attention to herself.

'I want to go for a pee-pee, Mummy,' she said.

'Good girl,' said Margaret. 'Off you go to the bathroom.'

Michelle's bid to claim the stage had failed so she made an even bolder attempt to get noticed. 'But I want to do the pee-pee in the sink, Mummy,' she said.

That got her Margaret's undivided attention as, full of embarrassment, she rushed her off to the bathroom.

I dearly love my three children and one of my punishments before a fight is that I refuse to see them from the moment I leave for London until the contest is over. They soften me up too much and I like to make myself mean and moody for a fight. I also never touch my guitar while I'm in training. Everything that gives me pleasure is put out of my mind while I give the contest and my opponent my total and undivided attention. Boxing is a long, lonely slog, for both Margaret and me.

There has, of course, been a lot of consolation and compensation for the pressures put on our marriage by the demands of boxing. The rewards in the last two years of my career have been excellent and we have been able to afford a fashionable home in Kirkintilloch and I am now able to keep my family in the manner to which I want them to become accustomed. My money is hard-earned and the canny Scot in me will see that it is wisely spent.

I owe it all to the unfairly maligned sport of boxing and to Terry Lawless, who gave me a new style and a new attitude.

Round 4

The Champion Maker

The first thing Terry Lawless did to get me to change my style of boxing was tie me up. He felt that I was not getting full power into my punches because I had too wide a stance. So to get me to bring my feet closer together he looped string around my ankles and then made me move around the gym throwing punches at his hand pads.

It was in these early days with Terry that I began to realize just how little I really knew about boxing and I started to appreciate that he was not just a good manager but also an outstanding coach. He boxed only briefly as an amateur, but has a natural eye and feel for what a fighter needs to do in a ring.

In my first visit to his gymnasium he watched me spar with Sylvester Mittee, one of his outstanding protégés. After we had finished our work-out, Terry took me on one side and said: 'There are just a couple of suggestions I want to make that will make you a fifty per cent better fighter.' His opinion was that I was too negative with my style. 'You are putting too much weight on your back foot, your legs are too wide apart and your balance is wrong,' he said. It was pretty crushing criticism, but I couldn't argue with him. He said he wanted me to retain my defensive skills, but to add some aggression because he felt I had been getting unnecessarily involved in distance fights that I could have ended early with a different attitude and approach.

'You're a dream of a back-foot fighter,' he said. 'But if you're going to reach your full potential, you've got to be able to punch off your front foot. You need more leverage for your punches. At the moment you're doing nearly all your punching off the back foot and so your weight distribution is wrong when the punch lands. I want you to try stepping in with your punches, placing your weight firmly on your front foot and with your feet closer together. Your stance is so wide that you lack a complete mobility and you have been unable to shift your weight from your back foot.'

Now that I look back, I can appreciate that Terry was 100 per cent correct with his comments on my style. I *was* too cautious and defensive, mainly because I don't like getting hit. That distaste for taking punches remains with me and I still like to counterpunch and continue to do most of my work off the back foot. The difference is that thanks to Terry's coaching I can now step forward on to my front foot when I have an opponent in trouble and really punish him with heavy, 'full frontal' blows.

People often ask me if punches still hurt once you've got used to taking them. Well of course they do! I've been blessed with a strong jaw but I take as few punches as possible and am the founder and President of the Jim Watt Preservation Society. I am well aware of the risks involved in boxing. It is legalized violence and I know all the dangers that lurk inside that lonely roped square. But to the abolitionists I would say that nobody forces me to get into the ring. It's a calculated risk, just as motor racing, mountaineering, steeplechasing and any sport with an element of danger. In my case it's an *extremely* calculated risk because I'm a calculating sort of person who doesn't do anything without a lot of careful thought and consideration as to what's involved.

Without boxing I would be a nobody. The failures in our sport always make the headlines, but for every one that falls by the wayside there are a dozen or more for whom boxing has been the passport to a decent and honest way of life. It has given me an identity and sufficient money to provide for my wife, children and loved ones. You won't get me condemning the sport. It's a hard and hazardous way to make a living, but I do it of my own free will.

I became a much more positive and confident person under

Terry's guidance and his astonishing tactical knowledge of boxing gave me a whole new insight into a sport that I thought I knew well. His main strength apart from his coaching talent is his ability to motivate, particularly in the corner during a fight when the pressure is at its peak. He is like a psychiatrist with his boxers, knowing just what to say to lift them when the muscles and the mind are tiring. A lot of cornermen I know waste their breath by talking throughout the minute break. Terry saves his instructions for the last twenty seconds so that the points he wants to make stay in the boxer's mind. He never makes his corner advice complicated and will patiently repeat it two or three times to make sure you understand. No two boxers are treated the same in a Lawless corner. There are lazy ones who need bullying, nervous ones who need their confidence boosted, cocky ones who need bringing down a peg, and assured ones who need to be kept assured by quiet words of encouragement. I like to think I come in the last category.

Strictly speaking, cornermen are not allowed to shout instructions to a fighter during a contest. But those who abide by this rule could hold an AGM in a telephone box. I am always aware of Terry's shouted instructions no matter how loud the roar of the crowd. He shouts simple phrases that he uses during gym sparring such as 'Through the middle' (meaning he wants me to drive my left up through the middle of my opponent's defence), 'Clusters . . . clusters . . .' (combination punches of a five or six punch sequence), 'Back him up . . .' (force your opponent back), 'Step . . . step . . .' (take a half step forward so that I am punching with full power off my front foot), 'Tuck up . . .' (tuck my chin into my right shoulder and keep my guard high to present as small a target as possible).

Terry is the most meticulous and professional person I know. He gives enormous attention to detail and what I particularly like about his style of management is that he doesn't think his job is finished once the final bell has rung. He continues to give full consideration to his boxer, win or lose, and nurses him for the rest of the evening until he is ready to leave the arena.

There is never any attempt to delegate his duties and he insists on keeping his training team small and unchanged. He is very strong on loyalty and Frank Black and George Wiggs have both worked with him for years. There is not a better organized or smoother functioning team in the game. Another important team member is masseur Jim Middleton, whose magic hands manipulate life back into tired muscles after strenuous training sessions.

All the main jobs are done by Terry, who first learnt the art of cornerwork as an assistant to the vastly experienced Al 'Aldgate Tiger' Phillips in the mid-1950s. He is expert at taping and bandaging the hands of boxers. This is vital for me because right through my career I have suffered from severe knuckle bruising. Terry is also a master cuts man and works with the speed and efficiency of a surgeon in the corner. He does running repairs with a cotton swab stick, adrenalin and a vaseline mixture and seals wounds by pressing the cut together and then applying the adrenalin and vaseline to make the blood congeal. In the minute between rounds, he can work miracles on an injury. Frank Black concentrates on sponging the boxer down and massaging the muscles while George Wiggs makes sure the stool is swung into the ring at the exact second the bell rings, washes the gumshield and provides the water bottle which is filled before the fight and sealed so that nobody can 'nobble' it.

I have to report that 'The Lawless One' is not all sweetness and light. There is a rough side to this basically nice man. You don't get to the top in the jungle of world championship boxing without being able to hold your own in the political clinches. He is a very formidable opponent in shouting matches when there are complicated contracts to be negotiated. His stubbornness comes to the surface only on behalf of his boxers. I have overheard him tearing promoters to shreds when he has felt his boxers have been offered anything less than a fair deal.

Away from boxing, Terry ducks out of the limelight. He is a private person who likes to listen to good music, eat totally burnt steaks, drink good wine, read autobiographies and spend as much time at home with Sylvie, Stephen and

Lorraine as his busy schedule will allow. A book that comes near the top of the reading list for both Terry and me is the autobiography of W. C. Fields, *Never Give a Sucker an Even Break*.

The loyalty Terry looks for in boxing also spreads to his private life and I have noticed that his small band of close friends is made up mostly of people he has been associated with for twenty years or more. One of his best mates, even though they have divided interests, is top amateur boxing coach Tony Burns, of the famous Repton club in London's East End. They get along fine provided they don't talk about their two different codes of boxing!

Another sports character close to Terry is Manchester United manager Dave Sexton, whose father, Archie, was rated the greatest middleweight never to win a British championship. Dave is a keen supporter of all Lawless fighters and is very much like Terry in personality and in his totally professional and dedicated approach to his sport.

Terry laughs easily and makes the people around him laugh easily. But he is a sleeping tiger and when aroused on boxing matters can make people quake in their boots with words that are dropped like hand grenades. There is a procession of pressmen that I could call as witnesses to the fact that the one thing Terry cannot cope with is criticism of any of his boxers. He has a good relationship with the media but is quick to give any of them a verbal volley if they have the temerity to knock one of his boys.

Some cynics seem to consider Terry a satellite in the whirling world of Mickey Duff, the most persuasive and powerful man in European boxing and a match for anybody on the American scene. But I can vouch for the fact that Terry is very much his own man. He gives Mickey ulcers with his demands and is such a tenacious negotiator on behalf of his boxers that I think he really *could* get blood out of a stone. I have more, much more to tell about the remarkable Mickey Duff in a later chapter.

Never in the history of British boxing has there been a more successful manager than Terry Lawless, so his methods must be right. He is the only British manager to have guided three boxers to world championships (John H. Stracey, Maurice Hope and me) and his roll call of other champions include Jimmy Anderson, Ralph Charles, Charlie Magri, Jimmy Batten, Kirkland Laing, Ray Cattouse and John L. Gardner.

I will lay odds that before the 1980s are out he will have doubled that number of champions because his Royal Oak gymnasium is packed with young fighters of potential who have come seeking fame and fortune in the Terry Lawless Boxing Club. He makes it a rule never to approach contracted boxers and doesn't pay amateurs to turn professional with him. His argument is that once a manager pays a boxer a signing-on fee, his mind is set more on recouping the money than making sure the boy is properly matched and brought along at the right pace. You never see a Lawless boxer rushed to the top.

For such a well-organized and professional person, Terry is sometimes strangely anchored by superstition. There is no logic to it but he always insists on following exactly the same routine before a fight, down to his boxers using the same dressing-room and the same ring corner for visits to regular venues like the Royal Albert Hall and Wembley. Everybody knows that only he must open the telegrams in the dressing-room and he is never completely happy until he has seen one arrive from one of his closest pals Norman Giller, the writer who has helped me get these words down on paper. He and Terry have been going through the telegram routine for more than a dozen years and have become completely hooked on the superstition. Terry thought the superstition had been broken when Maurice Hope fought for the world light-middleweight title in San Remo. He got really agitated before the fight because Norman's telegram had not arrived, but Maurice went out and won in style. When Terry returned to his hotel he found the telegram pushed under the door of his room. The superstitious forces were re-activated. It is also part precaution when Terry stresses that only he must open the telegrams. Nuts have been known to send telegrams to fighters with messages such as HOPE YOU DROP DEAD.

Few top-line sportsmen are without at least some small superstition. I always make a point of having my hair cut by an old friend of ours, Hugo Patriarco, at his Walthamstow salon before each major fight. The most illogical thing I do is to buy a roll of pink tape for my bandages; I know Terry will refuse to use it because it's the wrong colour. Whenever one of Terry's boxers becomes a champion he buys them a small gold boxing glove to wear on a chain around the neck. Ever since I joined this exclusive club I've never been without it and before each fight I give the glove to Frank Black to wear so that I know it's in the corner with me. Terry and I lean heavily on Lady Luck but the real reason for our success together has been our thoroughly professional approach to every fight. Once that bell rings you make your own luck.

From the outside the Royal Oak, Canning Town, looks just another east London pub. But when you go through the side door and climb the narrow staircase to the first floor you enter another world. This is where Terry Lawless has his gymnasium. The Academy of Boxing. I am sure there is no gymnasium like it anywhere in the world.

Too many gyms are like Wild West duelling locations. Sparring sessions become wars as boxers foolishly try to prove themselves kings of the gym. Some of my hardest fights have been in Glasgow gymnasiums where sparring partners have wanted to prove their superiority. I have often had to be spiteful with my punches to put them in their place. You never see ring wars at the Royal Oak. Terry Lawless insists that the gym is a place for learning and conditioning *not* for collecting the scalps of sparring partners. His rule is that you must spar not scar.

The first thing that hits you when you walk through the double doors into the Royal Oak gymnasium is the wall of heat. There is a well-stoked boiler going at full power throughout the boxing season and it turns the room into a real sweat shop. With as many as a dozen boxers working out in an area no bigger than the floor of a double garage, the heat generated can be almost suffocating for anybody not accustomed to it.

The second thing that strikes you is that there is a lot of

laughter in the air for a place populated by so many supposedly mean men. Humour crackles through the steamy heat
as we try to score points off each other.

I remember in one of my early visits when a ceiling strip
light started flashing on and off. Terry gave it a jab with a
broomhandle and the temperamental light then worked perfectly. Terry flashed a smile at Maurice Hope, whose black
face was soaked with bubbles of perspiration following a
sequence of explosive exercises.

'White man, he heap clever,' he said to Maurice in pidgin
English. 'Make light work with magic stick.'

'B'wana, him miracle maker,' Maurice said. 'Him make me
see the light.'

There's not a hint of racial tension in the gym where black,
white, Irish, Scots, Catholic, Protestant, the long, the short
and the tall all mix together in a harmony that gives the gym a
family atmosphere. It's the Terry Lawless Boxing Club and
all his boxers are proud to be members.

Terry rules the gym with a velvet glove but it hides an iron
fist for anybody stepping out of line. I know of two top-line
boxers that he was happy to let go because their attitude was
upsetting the Royal Oak team spirit, and he once briefly
suspended British champions Jimmy Batten and Kirkland
Laing from the gym after they had allowed a sparring session
to spill over into an angry war. In most gyms it would have
been accepted as the norm. But not in the Lawless Academy.

I believe in turning my training for each fight into a
personal punishment. My ground work is done in Glasgow
where I supervise my own training and make it a competition
between my mind and my body. My body reaches a point
where it is aching to give up, but my mind demands greater
effort. I never feel satisfied until I am totally exhausted. If I do
twenty press-ups one day, I make sure I do twenty-five the
next, thirty the next, and so on. In Glasgow I have a regular
sparring companion called Hughie Smith, an accomplished
pro who has become my good pal despite the fact that we have
punched each other on the nose hundreds of times in training.
We help each other prepare for fights and I reckon Hughie
knows my style better than anybody.

When I'm training myself, I drive myself to the limit and beyond and usually go too far, but I know that when I go down to join Terry in London about a month before each fight he will take over and balance things out. It's a relief to join Terry at the Royal Oak and let him carry the burden of making decisions about training, sparring, when to work, when to rest, when to eat and sleep. Suddenly I am free of the responsibility of family and business decisions and I can just give total concentration to the fight ahead.

I look forward to meeting up again with my colleagues in the Terry Lawless Boxing Club where I always feel at home. We are all set a series of punishing training schedules, with Terry supervising and coaching, somehow finding time to give every one of his boxers personal attention. He is helped by trainer Frank Black and loyal assistant George Wiggs, both of whom are invaluable and popular members of the club.

We all respect Frank but use him as a target for many of our jokes. He is a former professional footballer who has lived in England for more than thirty years, but sounds as Irish now as when he left his hometown of Dublin as a youngster. All the current Irish jokes are twisted round and aimed at Frank who enjoys them as much as we do. ('Did you hear about the Irish boxing trainer who demonstrated the Ali Shuffle with a pack of cards? When he went to the Boxing Board of Control for his licence he was told to fill in the questionnaire, so he beat up the doorman. . . . We draw him a diagram so that he knows which corner to work in during the fight. . . . Before he puts our gloves on for sparring we mark an L on the right one and an R on the left one because we know he'll get them wrong. . . .'

Frank takes all this sort of stick in his stride and usually has a dig back. When I was preparing for one of my world title defences, he said to me all straight-faced: 'You tink oi'm a tick Mick, but what does that make you? When the bell rings for the foight oi get out of the ring and you have to stay in there. . . .' There is no answer to that.

Frank is an ideal right-hand man for Terry and the way he allows himself to be used as a butt for so many jokes helps give the gymnasium its magic atmosphere.

When my fighting is finally done, I shall always look back on my visits to the Royal Oak gym with great nostalgia. The fact that I was made to feel welcome there right from the start of my new career with Terry helped boost my confidence and ambition. Nearly everybody in the gym has a title of some kind, but there are no big heads and if anybody does show signs of getting too cocky, he is quickly cut down to size by the wickedly sharp humour on which you could cut yourself.

My closest pal among my stablemates is the one to whom I have had least to say, Maurice Hope. Mo and I get on really well, yet we don't talk to each other all that much. We could go on a journey from, say, London to Glasgow hardly exchanging a word and yet thoroughly enjoying each other's company. I like his dry sense of humour and his easy-going West Indian manner. He shrugs his muscular shoulders and takes what ever comes in his stride. When a detached retina threatened his career soon after he had become world champion, he controlled his emotions with great dignity and said: 'I'll go along with whatever the Man Up There decides. But just remember that where there's hope there's life.'

Maurice Hope. I love him like a brother. *That's* the sort of family spirit we have in the Terry Lawless Boxing Club.

It would take a Cockney Damon Runyan to capture some of the characters who come into the gym, like Jimmy Flint – the Wapping Assassin – who has got a wicked left hook and eyes that drill right through opponents. Then there is tiny Charlie Magri off whom we bounce a lot of our jokes. He barely weighs eight stone dripping wet and Terry sits him on his knee like a ventriloquist's dummy and pretends to feed him with a baby bottle. But Charlie is nobody's dummy. He is as bright as a button and one of the most devastating box-fighters I've ever seen.

Of all the characters my favourite is Jim the Biscuit, so called because he is a biscuit salesman. He has recently taken on a new alias, Jim the Plum, because he is forever coming into the gymnasium handing out plums that he has grown in his garden. Jim is a regular spectator at the gym and is the king of the jibbers. He travels the world to watch boxing, always paying his way. But at the end of the journey he considers it almost a matter of principle that he will get one of the best seats in the house without parting with the ticket money. I particularly remember one night in Madrid when I was defending my European lightweight title against Perico Fernandez. The Biscuit had filled a bucket with ice and was going to walk into the arena with Terry, Frank Black, George Wiggs and me as if he were one of the seconds. But his plan collapsed when Jimmy Batten swiped his bucket and used it to get himself through the officials' entrance. The Biscuit wasn't beaten. He saw Margaret, Sylvie Lawless and Theresa Batten about to enter the arena and made a great fuss of ushering them through the crowd. He is always elegantly attired and wears a bow tie that gives him a dignified look. Everybody made way in gentlemanly manner as Jim ushered the ladies past the ticket collector and right down to the second row of the ringside where they had reserved seats.

The Biscuit then audaciously sat himself down in a front row press seat. A steward asked to see his ticket and Jim, with a dramatic flourish, produced a timekeeper's stopwatch from his top pocket. The steward was most impressed and there was quite a commotion while he insisted on some journalists transferring their seats. Jim the Biscuit was then shown into a seat alongside the official timekeeper. At the end of the fifteen rounds, the referee collected the scorecards of the judges and handed them to The Biscuit for checking! He went to the extreme of querying one of the rounds and finally passed them as okay once he had satisfied himself that I was the winner. As it happened I had won the fight by a mile, but I would not have put it past Jim to have added a few points if he had found that any of the judges had me behind.

From the moment I joined Terry he started badgering the big London promoters for work. They needed me on their shows like a landlord needs dry rot, but Terry can be very very persuasive. I had my first fight under his management against George Turpin of Liverpool on a Mike Barrett–Mickey Duff

promotion at the Royal Albert Hall on 2 March 1976. I was in
and out of the show like a fiddler's elbow as matchmaker Duff
juggled with a bill that kept collapsing on him. Finally, I was
booked to fight Turpin in a replacement contest for a
heavyweight showdown between Richard Dunn and Earnie
Shavers. I don't think the public could have been too pleased
and one newspaper summed it up with the headline: JIM WHO
TOPS THE BILL.

Turpin had been a top-class amateur, winning the ABA
bantamweight title and an Olympic bronze medal at the 1972
Munich Games. He was unbeaten in ten professional fights,
but I was too big and experienced for him as he made his first
step up into the lightweight division. Our styles clashed and it
was an untidy affair until I found my timing and distance in
the fourth round. I then went to work with my new front-foot
power and had him down four times before referee Sid Nathan
counted him out. All my old confidence and ambition started
bubbling again and at last I felt as if I had been properly
launched in London.

Three weeks later I was in action again, this time in a
non-title fight against Anglo-Scot Jimmy Revie at London's
Cunard Hotel. Revie was a former British featherweight
champion and a determined and skilful ring technician. I had
made this match myself, negotiating terms with promoter
Paddy Byrne at £850 before Terry became my manager. Terry
agreed to let me go through with the fight, although I sensed
he didn't think I had done a particularly good deal considering I was meeting such a talented opponent. So much for my
efforts at self-management! There was an unsatisfactory end
to a cracking fight when Revie was led back to his corner in
the seventh round with a bad cut over his right eye. I felt
that I had a decisive edge in the fight, but would liked to
have made my victory more emphatic against a top-class
rival.

Terry kept drumming it into me about being positive. He
had discovered a fact that I have always tried to hide and that
is that deep down I have an inferiority complex. I fear failure
as a deadly disease and am always secretly worried about
letting myself down in the ring. But Terry kept chipping away

at my complex and concentrated on building up my confidence. His demands that I should be more aggressive paid off in my third fight for him when I pounded Hector Diaz, of the Dominican Republic, to defeat in four rounds at the Anglo-American Sporting Club at the Hilton Hotel. Mickey Duff came into my dressing-room after the victory and told me: 'I've always known you've got what it takes to go right to the top and Terry has found a way of bringing your great talent to the surface. Keep this sort of form up and you'll soon be champion of Europe.'

That was praise from the top of the mountain. But five weeks after this May fight I felt as if I was back in the foothills. Johnny Claydon caught me with a head butt in the second round of our non-title fight at Wembley Arena on the night of 22 June 1976. I had been in command against the fighter from West Ham, but knew I was in trouble the moment his head hit me. Blood streamed from a cut at the side of my right eye and even Terry's expert repair work was to no avail. Claydon re-opened the injury with the first punch of the third round and referee Roland Dakin led me back to my corner with a cut eye for the second time in a vital fight. He had stopped my championship contest with Willie Reilly four years earlier at Nottingham Ice Rink. Each time his decision was correct.

I have rarely known a more depressing night in boxing. Within an hour my stablemate John Stracey had been relieved of the world welterweight championship by Carlos Palomino. Our dressing-room, usually alive with bright faces and laughter, was like a funeral parlour. The Stracey setback was a severe blow for British boxing in general and for Terry and John in particular. It was no time for me to be seeking sympathy and I hurried away from Wembley with my business partner Arthur Morrison who had to put up with my black mood all the way home to Glasgow.

Terry contacted me first thing the next day and said: 'We will turn this setback to our advantage. Claydon will now want a return with the title at stake. This will give you the golden opportunity to achieve your ambition of winning a Lonsdale Belt outright.'

Fired by this positive thinking, I hammered Italian Franco

49

Diana to defeat in six rounds at Wembley on 12 October 1976, and – just as Terry had figured – I was matched with Claydon for the championship at St Andrew's Sporting Club four months later on 21 February 1977.

Claydon and I had some bitter moments during the fight. I got angry with him because there were at least five occasions when I sensed he was trying to catch me with his head, as had happened in our previous fight. But after referee Wally Thom had stopped it in the tenth round to save Claydon from further punishment, I had as much respect for him as I have ever had for an opponent. He showed courage beyond the call of duty, getting off the canvas four times to try to stay in the fight.

I was over Mars (I nearly said the moon but I'll leave that cliché for the footballers) at the end because I had achieved my long-time ambition of winning a Lonsdale Belt outright. I shall treasure it all my life.

Terry Lawless was thoughtful enough to tell the press afterwards that Jim Murray deserved a lot of the credit because I had got the first two notches on the Belt when I was managed by him. But it was Lawless, the Champion Maker, who had given me my new lease of life. I now had a bigger ambition and a new target: to become champion of Europe.

Round 5

The Big Gamble

I surrendered the British championship in the summer of 1977 rather than defend it against Northern Ireland challenger Charlie Nash in his hometown of Derry. The fight would have brought me a then best-ever pay day of £8000. I was tempted by the purse and the opponent but not the territory.

Terry Lawless wisely advised me to relinquish the title. 'It would only take one nut in the crowd to spark off something that nobody could control,' he reasoned. 'With the present situation in Northern Ireland I hardly think it would be wise for a Protestant Scot to fight an Irish Catholic at a Derry arena.'

It angered me that the British Boxing Board of Control were giving me an ultimatum either to go to Northern Ireland to fight or give up my title. I am a professional and fear no man in the ring, but I have a wife and family to consider when making decisions and there was no way I was going to risk anything happening to me in what was at the time a virtual war zone. Margaret was pregnant and I wanted to give her as little to worry about as possible.

There were stupid suggestions made that I was frightened of fighting Nash. Two previous fight dates with him had fallen through, one because I had a damaged back and the other following a contractual dispute. In my heart I knew that Charlie's style of fighting was tailor-made to suit me, but my head ruled that it would be madness to fight him in Ulster where religious feelings were running dangerously high.

In the meantime I had been nominated to meet my old French foe, André Holyk, for the vacant European championship and Terry decided we should make this our prime target and let the British title go. To enable St Andrew's Sporting Club matchmaker Les Roberts to win the bid for the bout, Terry and I agreed to a deal in which we would 'fight on the gate'. This meant we would only earn if the promotion showed a profit. It was the gamble of a lifetime because if I lost I would be virtually finished as a top-line contender and the one card that I held, the British title, had been given away along with a guaranteed purse of £8000. Terry has since admitted to me that he was worried sick in case anything went wrong against Holyk. 'I would have cost you £8000 and your British title and you would have wondered what kind of manager I was,' he said. 'Mind you, I would always have done the same thing again rather than let you fight in Northern Ireland at that time and in that atmosphere.' What Terry didn't know was that I was also worried sick before the fight with Holyk in case I let *him* down. I felt as if I had given him nothing but problems since joining him and he had hardly earned a penny piece for all the time and effort he had put in on my behalf.

As it happened, he didn't earn anything from the Holyk fight either. It was an August promotion and so many club members were away on holiday that the show failed to clear overheads. At the end of the evening there was no money left in the kitty for me. But the important thing was that we had won the European title and I hardly had to break sweat doing it.

The fight was all over in only eighty-two seconds. We had just one sharp exchange of punches and he broke away from a clinch with blood spurting from a deep gash on his right eyebrow. There was no way the contest could continue and Holyk cried with sheer frustration as he was led back to his corner. I was completely stunned by the suddenness of it all and felt sorry for the spectators who had hardly got value for their money. They didn't know what had happened – and neither did I. Holyk said I caused the damage with my head, adding that he thought it was accidental. But I certainly didn't feel any contact of heads and with my track record for cuts I would surely have been the one to bleed. As Ken Buchanan, the former title holder, presented me with the European championship belt, I satisfied myself with the thought that justice had been done because there was no doubt that I had been robbed of a points decision against Holyk when we had last met in Lyons.

At a celebration party in the Albany Hotel afterwards Margaret got high on a mixture of relief and wine and drifted off into a deep sleep the moment we went to our room in the wee small hours of the morning. I was so keyed up with excess energy that I couldn't keep my eyes closed and in those fitful moments you have in the no-man's-land between sleeping and waking I began to wonder if perhaps I had dreamt becoming champion of Europe. To reassure myself I got out of bed and took the European belt from its box and clasped it around my waist. For ten minutes I just stood looking at myself in the wardrobe mirror and reflecting on the Napoleonic feeling of being the boxing emperor of Europe.

Still I wasn't satisfied and I quietly got dressed and went downstairs to the banqueting suite where the fight had been staged just to make sure the ring was there. Sydney Hulls, *Daily Express* boxing correspondent and well-known gourmet, saw me as he came down from his room for breakfast.

'Just got up, Jim?' he asked.

'No, I'm just off to bed,' I said and then went out of the back exit of the hotel and walked the streets of Glasgow for an hour. I had been trained and wound up for a fifteen round fight and needed to take some sort of exercise to try to bring myself down to earth.

I didn't finish completely out of pocket after all. Lawrence Goodman, a valued friend of mine who helps to mastermind the St Andrew's Sporting Club promotions, later made a generous donation towards my training expenses. It cemented the close rapport I have always had with St Andrew's members since I topped their first-ever bill against Ken Buchanan. The club has done a marvellous job keeping boxing ticking over in Glasgow and without their enthusiasm and interest the game might have rolled over and died in Scotland.

There was world title talk in the air and I knew I dare not slip up in my first defence of the European crown against Spaniard

53

Jeronimo Lucas at the Midlands Sporting Club in Solihull on 16 November 1977. I boxed cautiously for the first few rounds and once I had found my range against an awkward opponent started to put together combination punches that continually stopped him in his tracks. As well as physical force I used psychological pressure on Lucas. Just before the bell at the beginning of every round I gave him a long hard stare, as much as to say, 'You're just here for the pay day, sunshine. This title belongs to *me*'. I knew I had him beaten after about five rounds when he couldn't return my stare. While it was my blows to the head that were taking the eye of the spectators, I was knocking the fight out of him with clusters of punches to the body. I was really sinking my punches in and Terry told me in the corner: 'I can hear him wincing every time you dig in to the body. He can't take it down there.' The Spaniard was fighting under the handicap of a cut left eye from the seventh round and when he shook his head sorrowfully at the end of the ninth I knew he would not be around much longer. I piled on the pressure in the tenth and the referee stopped the one-sided action after Lucas had taken a standing count of eight.

When I was asked after the fight if Lucas had worried me at any time during the contest, I said: 'There was just once in the fourth round when he caused me some concern. I nearly missed him a couple of times!' I felt guilty as soon as I had made the crack because Lucas had put up a brave show and I think it is unprofessional to knock an opponent after a fight. I eased my conscience by sorting out an interpreter and telling Lucas through him that he had been a credit to his country and to his sport.

Lucas was asked how he rated his countryman Perico Fernandez, who was the official No. 1 challenger for my European title. He winced and puffed out his cheeks to signify that Señor Fernandez was very hot stuff indeed. I would soon find out for myself exactly what he meant.

Round 6

The Fight of My Life

Terry Lawless and I had been in partnership for just under two years when he telephoned me with what he considered was bad news. 'I'm sorry, Jim,' he said, 'but we've lost the bid for the Fernandez fight. You'll be paid a purse of £12,000 to defend the title in Madrid.'

Twelve thousand pounds! I could hardly keep the smile off my face as I told Terry: 'Och, that's a shame.'

My attitude at that time was to get one big pay day and really cash in on the title. I had not yet got around to sharing Terry's total belief that I could become world champion.

We had hoped that Mickey Duff could clinch the fight for Britain but because he failed to get the backing of Scottish Television his bid fell short of the £21,000 put up by the Spanish promoters. On a 60–40 split, it meant my share of the purse would be £12,600. I was delighted.

Even though I held the title, I would be going into the fight as the underdog. Fernandez was a former world light-welterweight champion who was famed and feared for his punching power. He was a one-shot merchant who could take opponents out with a punch from either hand. Terry and I studied film of him in action and planned a campaign in which I would pressurize Fernandez and not give him time or room to set himself for his big punches. I trained to peak condition and when I left for Madrid, followed by a band of twenty loyal supporters, I felt as confident as I had ever been in my career.

Fernandez was convinced this was the fight he couldn't lose. He was the playboy pin-up idol of Spanish sport, with a glamorous filmstar wife and a lifestyle that continually kept him in the headlines. On my arrival in Spain I could see it in the face of every Spaniard I met that the fight was all won bar the punching. They rated me a cardboard champion. Jim Who?

I went on Spanish television with Fernandez for a pre-fight interview. On our way to the studio Terry told me: 'Everybody thinks we're a couple of country cousins here for a pay day and nothing else. Let Fernandez do all the talking on television to pump everybody's confidence even higher, then at the end of the interview you sign off by saying very clearly so that your interpreter gets it right, 'I am not here to surrender my title. Tomorrow night you are all going to get a hell of a shock.' Keep it that simple so that it sinks in. It will be the first time that anybody's mentioned even the remotest possibility of their hero losing.'

Later on at a press conference Terry and I worked together at getting a big psychological advantage over Fernandez. We knew he must be tight at the weight as he was stepping down a division and the one thing a fighter making weight must watch is his intake of liquids. I had experienced it when I was an amateur and it's torture. I was on a strict diet of a few sips of tea and I used to lie in bed at night thinking of huge glasses of ice-cold lemonade. This was the sort of agony Fernandez would have been suffering before our fight.

As Fernandez and I sat down alongside each other for the press conference Terry stepped forward with a bottle of iced mineral water and a glass which he put on the table between us. Then he slowly poured me a glassful of water. I could sense Fernandez fidgeting uncomfortably as he stared at the glass which I deliberately left untouched for a couple of minutes. Then I reached forward and drank it down in one go without the water touching the sides of my throat. No Glaswegian has ever sunk a pint with greater relish. Terry then refilled the glass and left the bottle temptingly right in front of Fernandez. There was no way I was going to drink any more because otherwise I would have been pushing myself above the weight limit, but the psychological damage had been done. Fernandez, no doubt weakened by his weight-reducing efforts, knew that he was getting into the ring with a champion who had no weight worries whatsoever. The press conference lasted twenty minutes, but must have seemed like twenty hours to the Spaniard, who just couldn't take his eyes off that ice-cold water bottle.

During the conference, Fernandez unwittingly gave me an extra incentive to give him a good hiding. He called me an Englishman!

On the afternoon of the fight I was relaxing in my hotel room when my good friends Jim Reynolds, of the *Glasgow Herald*, and Dick Currie, of the *Daily Record*, came to see me. They have reported my career since my early amateur days and we have a close relationship that goes beyond the usual sportsman–reporter association. Their visit was supposed to cheer me up and take my mind off the fight, but I could see by the long look on Jim's face that he was very concerned for my welfare. In fact he looked worried to death and had obviously been taken in by all the pre-fight ballyhoo from Fernandez, who made no secret of his plan to destroy me in double-quick time. For the next twenty minutes we had the crazy situation of me having to give Jim a pep talk and trying to cheer *him* up! I revealed my fight strategy and explained how I intended to prevent Fernandez from getting room in which to manoeuvre and settle himself for big punches. Jim listened intently and considered all that I had to say and then, his face still as sad as an untidy grave, said: 'Aye, Jim, I know what ye mean, but Fernandez has got such great big bloody hands!' I just exploded with laughter and let Jim get on with his pessimistic mood.

Getting to the ring for the contest was almost as hard as the fight itself. The long walk from the dressing-room was a nightmare and luckily I had Terry, Frank Black, George Wiggs and my stablemates Maurice Hope and Jimmy Batten to form a protective cordon around me. Spectators spat and jeered at me and a couple of times I was punched on the shoulders. Terry had managed winning fighters in Mexico, Munich, Rome, Paris, Brisbane, Zürich and all points west and gave me a tight smile as we climbed into the ring. 'That's the hardest part over,' he said. 'You watch the way they cheer you out.'

I looked down at the ringside and caught Margaret's eye. She was sitting with Sylvie Lawless and Theresa Batten. I had advised her to stay at home because she was seven months pregnant, but she said she would worry less if she was at the ringside rather than sitting at home waiting for news of the fight. She forced a smile and gave me a wave, but later admitted that she was feeling terrified.

The fans went berserk as Fernandez came bouncing into the ring and gave a victory salute to all four corners of the arena. Now I knew how the poor bull must feel when he is all alone in a Spanish bullring. Jim Reynolds was positioned right beneath us in the first row of the press seats. I gestured to Terry to look at him and said: 'Do you think he'll last the fifteen rounds?' He looked like a man attending his own funeral.

Fernandez had scored five first-round victories in his career and came tearing out determined to make me short-cut victim No. 6. He was whirlwinding his punches at me and late in the round he caught me with a left-right combination to the side of the head and down I went. That was supposed to have been it. All over. When Fernandez drops 'em, they stay dropped – so the legend went.

I was more embarrassed than hurt and instinctively went to get straight up, but professionalism came to my rescue and I spun round on my knees to look towards my corner from where, at the count of eight, Terry signalled me to get up. The bell went soon after and I was in complete control of myself as I walked back to the corner. Jim Reynolds looked in a sorrier state than I did as I reached my stool. I threw him a wink and shouted: 'Don't worry. I'll be all right.' He later told me that when I went down he was in the process of drawing a fifteen-round schedule for his notes. As I hit the canvas he threw away his pencil in despair! There was an even more dramatic reaction from Margaret, who fled from the ringside with Sylvie Lawless in close pursuit. Sylvie watched the rest of the fight from the back of the arena, giving Margaret a blow-by-blow commentary through a half-open door.

A television cameraman with a hand-held miniature camera climbed onto the ring apron and the next thing I knew an interviewer was sticking a microphone in my face and asking in fractured English how I felt. Action spoke louder than words as Terry lashed out with his foot and told him, impolitely, to remove himself forthwith or words to that effect.

'You've already broken his heart, Jim,' Terry said as he sponged my face. 'He couldn't believe it when you got up. Now don't give him the opportunity to catch you again. Keep him on the end of that right jab. You can't miss him with it.'

The next fourteen rounds became carbon copies of each other. I knocked all the fight and resistance out of Fernandez, who kept falling back onto the ropes and covering up while I took pot shots every time I saw an opening. I punished him to the body until I could hear him gasping for breath and forced him to take three standing counts of eight.

His fans became so quiet that I could hear every word of advice being shouted from the corner by Terry. Everything he shouted I tried, and the fight became almost like a training session. The Spaniard's corner realized that I was tuned in to Terry's instructions and sent a 16-stone giant round to our corner to hover menacingly near Terry and to try to block his vision. He would have been better employed trying to protect Fernandez from me. I gave him a mother and the father of a hiding and for the last third of the fight the crowd were on my side and chanting what I later learned was the Spanish word for 'coward' at their fallen idol. He was anything but a coward and took his punishment like a man. Before the fight Terry had protested at the choice of Italian referee Dino Ambrosini who had once robbed Maurice Hope of a world championship victory. But there was no way he could have scored this one against me. I was the first British boxer to win a European title fight in Spain where Alan Rudkin (twice), Ken Buchanan and Jack Bodell had been among the fighters who had been beaten – some of them robbed – in championship fights.

It was described in the trade paper *Boxing News* as the most convincing points victory ever achieved by a British boxer on the Continent and, as Terry had predicted, the Spanish fans cheered me all the way back to the dressing-room as I was

59

carried shoulder high by my ecstatic Scottish fans. Maurice Hope was sitting in the corner of the dressing-room when I got back and said with that famous poker face look of his: 'What kept you so long, man?'

For the next three hours I sat with my hands dipped in ice buckets. They were bruised and swollen from where I had been hitting Fernandez. I rated it the fight of my life and from that night on I had all the confidence in the world and began to believe what Terry Lawless had been saying for months. I *could* become champion of the world.

To keep me ticking over, Terry fixed me up with a ten-round non-title fight against Welsh champion Johnny Wall at the National Sporting Club on 12 June 1978. Wall announced his retirement the week before the contest and his countryman Billy Vivian was brought in as a substitute. There was some controversy over the choice of opponent, some people claiming that Vivian should not have been allowed in the ring with me. The Board of Control instructed that the fight should be cut to eight rounds. I found it a very difficult contest because I was on a hiding to nothing. A world title fight was just around the corner and a defeat at that stage would have proved disastrous. So I took no chances against Vivian, who fought well above himself and was in no way outclassed or humiliated. I coasted to a comfortable eight-round points victory and joined in the loud and deserved applause Vivian received at the end of the fight from the knowledgeable National Sporting Club members.

There was now just one more barrier between me and a crack at the world championship – yet another Spaniard, this one called Antonio Guinaldo. I was ordered to defend my European title against him and the fight went out to purse offers. Enter Mickey Duff.

Round 7

Lead on Mick Duff

Terry Lawless and Mickey Duff work together like a tandem team when there is a major fight to be made. For the Guinaldo contest, Mickey didn't want to do any of the pedalling. In fact, he wanted to promote the fight like he wanted a hole in his wallet. Too many commercial shows had died a death in Scotland for Mickey to be interested in the fight and he knew it wouldn't draw breath in London. 'I'm sorry, Terry,' he said, 'but this is one contest I couldn't sell. The way boxing is in Glasgow at the moment it would be easier to sell freezers to Eskimos.'

Now, if there's anybody in this world who *could* sell freezers to Eskimos, it's Mickey Duff, so Terry shrugged off his indifference and kept nagging at him to make a bid for the fight. It was too expensive a contest to be staged by a private club and the last thing we wanted was to have to go back to Spain for a defence.

In the week before the deadline for purse offers to be placed with the European Boxing Union, Mickey joined the Lawless family for a summer holiday on the Adriatic. Terry turned Mickey's holiday into a nightmare by bringing the fight into every conversation. 'I didn't give him a second's peace,' Terry told me later. 'On the beach, in the restaurant, in taxis . . . no matter where we were, I kept pumping away at him until it reached the point where he yelled at me, "You're ruining my holiday!"'

Finally, with just an hour to go to the deadline, Mickey had what he later described as a brainstorm and telephoned his associate Rodolfo Sabatini in Rome and instructed him to put in a written offer for the fight on his behalf. Mickey's bid was £15,100.

A couple of hours later he got a telephone call back from Rome and told Terry with a long face, 'I've just had terrible news.'

Terry, fearing the worst, said, 'You didn't get the fight?'

'Worse than that. My bid was the top one. I *have* got the bloody fight!' Mickey replied.

Mickey and his promotions partner Mike Barrett then showed their skill as entrepreneurs. They booked the Kelvin Hall, Glasgow, sold the fight for live showing on BBC Television, set up a sponsorship deal with Seiko and generated enough publicity to whip up interest that attracted a near-capacity crowd despite the fact that Rangers were playing at Ibrox in a European Cup tie on the same night. It was the night and the fight that convinced us all that boxing could be made to boom again in Glasgow.

But at one stage I feared the fight wouldn't take place. Nine days before I was due to get into the ring I knocked a spinal joint out of place during training and had to walk round with a Groucho Marx crouch until top London specialist, Dr Ken Kennedy, put the joint back in place. Then I received some intensive treatment from West Ham United physiotherapist Robbie Jenkins. Everyone worked so hard to get the show off the ground that I was determined not to let them down.

The Kelvin Hall crowd got behind me with a fervour that made it sound as if they had brought the Hampden roar with them. It was all too much of an ordeal for Guinaldo, who had no answer to my two-fisted attacks. I softened him up with body punches and was rocking him with blows to the head in the fifth round when he suddenly raised his right arm and turned his back in surrender. The Spanish press, who had described Fernandez as a coward after taking a considerable bashing from me in Madrid, accepted Guinaldo's surrender as the honourable thing to do. It was for them the acceptable way to acknowledge that I was the better man.

Before the fight, Guinaldo had promised to win the European championship as a wedding present for his fiancée who was cheering him on from the ringside. Margaret had us all in fits as we were leaving Kelvin Hall after my victory when she said, very straight-faced: 'Oh well, she'll have to make do with a three-piece suite for a wedding present like everybody else!'

There is more political in-fighting in boxing than in the United Nations Assembly. I would be the first to admit that it is not always the best fighter who wins the world champion-ship so much as the one with the right connections. I have been lucky to have the intelligent guidance of Terry Lawless and the influential support of promoters Duff and Barrett. The actual fighting is only half the battle. But for shrewd management and muscle in the promotional world I would have bowed out of boxing in 1976 having hardly scratched the surface of the Big Time. I owe almost as much for the late success in my career to Mickey and Mike as I do to Terry. They put their money where their mouths are and boldly gambled on supporting me in Glasgow where promoters have been known to dig their own financial graves.

Mike Barrett is the ideal balance for the exuberant Duff. He is the epitome of the cool, sophisticated British businessman, has great organizational flair and is always flowing with exciting ideas. Mike allows Mickey to do the front-running, but gives expert back-up that makes their partnership one of the most powerful and successful in world boxing.

Now Mickey Duff on the other hand . . . well, he is the most fascinating person I have ever met. His life story is like something out of a Jeffrey Archer novel. He was born (I almost said christened) Morris Prager in Poland and came to London's East End at the age of eight, a move ahead of the Nazi invasion that ended with many of his relatives perishing in concentration camps.

The son, grandson and great-grandson of rabbis, Mickey revolted against family traditions and took up pugilism rather than theology. He was boxing professionally at the age of fifteen and, so that his parents wouldn't know, he used the ring name Mickey Duff which he borrowed from a character in a James Cagney film. After four years and an impressive record of sixty wins in sixty-nine fights, Mickey decided it would be more sensible to make the matches rather than fight in them. Here he *was* following family traditions because his mother had been a Jewish matrimonial matchmaker in Poland.

At the age of twenty he became the youngest licensed matchmaker in the world. That was in 1950 and in the last thirty years he has established himself on both sides of the Atlantic as one of the most influential figures in boxing. He has been involved in more than thirty world championship promotions, including several with Muhammad Ali. Mickey first promoted in Glasgow more than twenty years ago in partnership with former European bantamweight champion, Peter Keenan, who continues to be associated with all of Mickey's shows in Glasgow and does a valuable job keeping boxing alive in Scotland.

Mickey is a promoter, matchmaker, manager, adviser and has worked as a cornerman and trainer. He has also been known to pick up the microphone and do the ring MC's job. In short, he does like to be involved!

A born raconteur, he is the man with a million anecdotes and has a story for every occasion. One day he will get them down on paper and when put in some sort of order, they will surely add up to a best seller. I have never known anybody like him for travelling. He is always globetrotting and I think if he ever comes back to this world it will be as a pilot.

Of the thousand or so stories that Mickey has told me over the last few years, the one that made me laugh longest was about his days as a manager in the 1950s when he took three fighters over to Belfast to box. Mickey had specifically requested that his boxers be put on early so that they could catch the late-night ferry back to England. He erupted with anger when he discovered that one of his boys had been given the last spot on the show. Just as he was about to give the promoter a considerable piece of his mind, the boxer assured him: 'Don't worry, Mickey. I'll get the fight over and done with really quickly. We'll catch the ferry.'

The last fight of the night was over within thirty seconds. Mickey's boxer collapsed as if pole-axed from the first punch thrown by his opponent. When Mickey dived anxiously into the ring to remove his boxer's gumshield as he lay flat on his back, the fighter gave him a big wink and said: 'I told you we wouldn't miss the ferry!'

Mickey and Terry Lawless have a very close working relationship and also a well-cemented friendship that goes back more than twenty years. Yet despite their deep liking for each other's company, Mickey says that there's not a manager in the world who gives him a tougher time in fight negotiations than Terry.

It was Mickey's powers of persuasion and deep knowledge of boxing politics that helped swing me a world championship fight against Alfredo Pitalua, of Colombia. We heard on the boxing grapevine that the World Boxing Council were going to demote me from No. 2 contender for the title to No. 3, which would have left Pitalua and Andy Ganigan of Hawaii as the two top candidates for a world title fight, following the decision of champion Roberto Duran to step up to the light-welterweight division.

Mickey, Terry and British Boxing Board of Control Secretary, Ray Clarke, who does a great job protecting the interests of British fighters abroad, took my case for championship recognition to a WBC meeting in Nevada. They shot down the world's big guns in a tough political battle and came away with me reinstated as No. 2 contender for the championship.

Then Mickey was off on his travels to clinch the fight with Pitalua. His first stop was Miami where he paid flamboyant American promoter Don King $20,000 to release Pitalua from a previous contract. Next he went to Mexico City to agree terms with the Colombian fighter and finally flew to New York to try to set up a satellite television deal.

That was the *easy* part. He was gambling on a fight that was costing him and Mike Barrett a fortune. But where could they put it on?

Round 8

Champion of the World

We had the fight! Alfredo Pitalua *v*. Jim Watt for the light-weight championship of the world. Now we had to find an arena. Before flying to Miami and Mexico to clinch the contest, Mickey Duff told Terry Lawless there was little hope that he would be able to stage it in Glasgow.

'There's only Kelvin Hall,' he explained, 'and for the money this fight is going to cost us it just wouldn't be viable, certainly not with the present seating capacity. Our only chance would be if they would agree to increasing the number of seats.'

I was determined to fight for the title in front of my ain folk if at all possible and decided to seek local advice. I took two friends of mine, Govan Councillor Andy McMahon and Glasgow *Evening Times* boxing writer John Quinn, into my confidence and told them the situation.

'What,' I asked Andy McMahon, who is now an MP at Westminster, 'would be the correct procedure for approaching the Lord Provost about getting Glasgow interested in staging the fight?'

'That will be no problem,' Andy said. 'The Provost, David Hodge, just happens to be one of the most approachable people you could wish for and he is also a very knowledgeable fight fan.'

I kept John Quinn informed about what was happening because I wanted him ultimately to report exactly what went on in my meeting with the Provost so that the people of Glasgow would know how keen I was for the fight to be promoted in my home town. The Provost could not have been more helpful or enthusiastic when we went to see him. On

66

reflection, I realize how lucky I was that my championship challenge coincided with his period in office. He could remember the days when the large Kelvin Hall was regularly used for major fight promotions and publicly gave his backing to Andy McMahon's suggestion that extra seating should be installed to increase the capacity of the main arena. 'Jim Watt belongs to Glasgow and so does his world title fight,' said David Hodge. What a man!

John Quinn telephoned the news to Mickey Duff in Miami where he was negotiating with Don King for Pitalua's release from a contract. 'Marvellous!' said Mickey. 'If we get those extra seats in I'm confident we can get the fight for Glasgow.'

I attended a meeting at the Glasgow City Chambers with Councillors McMahon and John McQueenie, Director of Halls Tom Malarkey, and City Building Control officials Roy McGowan, Bob Dalgleish and Jim Wylie. We had a huge plan of the Kelvin Hall arena laid out on the conference table between us and worked out where 6000 extra seats could be placed. I was not exactly a stranger to this plan-reading exercise. The last time additional scaffolding seats had been installed at Kelvin Hall was for a police tattoo ten years earlier and I had been one of the electricians employed on necessary re-wiring. The big difference was that this time I was going to have to fill the seats.

The City Council passed the plan and Keith Fraser, secretary of the Glasgow Sports Promotion Council, announced that his organization was prepared to help meet the cost of putting in the extra seats. Glasgow had got right behind me and I will never ever forget their support.

When the Lord Provost announced at a press conference that, thanks to the City Fathers and the Sports Council, the world title fight would be staged in Glasgow on 17 April 1979, everybody started to celebrate as if the championship were already won. There was just the little matter of the fighting to be done and that was up to me.

Suddenly I felt as if I was having my head put in a noose as happened with Scotland football manager Ally MacLeod. Scotland's sad exit from the World Cup in Argentina was still fresh and heavy in the minds of all Scots. Ally had not been forgiven for the broken promises and now I sensed that everybody was looking at me to put some pride back into our sport.

I put extra pressure on myself with a business deal in which I committed myself to spending money that I did not have. In 1975 I had started a small car re-spraying concern with Arthur Morrison and we had expanded this to take in car repairs and servicing under the guidance of a good business pal of ours, Billy Blossom. Our present premises were scheduled to be demolished in a City redevelopment scheme and a couple of months before my world title fight against Pitalua, new premises came on the market for £72,000. I took a deep breath and pledged myself to spending the money. It was a deliberate act to give myself no room whatsoever for failure. I just dare not lose.

There was one other thing worrying me. How were we going to shift 10,000 tickets when the most we have previously had to sell was 2000? But within two weeks of the fight being announced, our chief ticketsellers, Arthur Morrison, Eddie Coakley and Peter and Cissie Keenan, were overwhelmed with inquiries and it was obvious that we were going to have a sell-out.

I had been almost bullying our regular punters to take three times as many tickets as usual. Suddenly we had the crazy situation where we couldn't meet their demands and I saw it as my duty to contact each one of them personally to apologize for not being able to provide as many tickets as we had promised. This brought me the rollicking that I needed from Walter McGowan, who had been a magnificent world flyweight champion back in the mid-1960s. When I telephoned him at his Carluke pub, he gave me a right telling-off. 'What are you doing worrying your head about tickets?' he said, the old boxing pro coming to the surface. 'The only thing you should be thinking of is the fight. The best thing you can do is get yourself out of Glasgow and away from the pressures, the back-slappers and the media.' I have always had a high regard for Walter and this wee man suddenly became ten feet tall in my eyes for the point-blank advice he had offered me. I was getting myself in too much of a flap over peripheral matters that should not have been any of my concern.

Six weeks before the fight I took a break from training and went to San Remo to watch my stablemate and friend Maurice Hope challenge for the world light-middleweight title. We never miss each other's major contests and I helped out in the corner as he battled to take the championship from Rocky Mattioli. It was fascinating and in a way frightening to watch Terry Lawless in action from the other side of the ropes. I didn't realize just how quickly that minute break between rounds flashes by and it was an education to see the way Terry handled the small crises that cropped up during the fight which would have made less experienced and less knowledgeable cornermen panic. My job was to look after the water bottle and make sure nobody tampered with it. Even that little chore was wearing and I almost applauded Terry for the way he coped. He is a real master in the corner.

Maurice was magnificent and was well on top when Mattioli retired at the end of the eighth round with a damaged hand. I could not have been more pleased had I just won the title and I gave Mighty Mo a victory cuddle in the ring. 'People will start talking about us, man,' he said.

A picture that has remained in my mind from that San Remo trip is of Maurice sitting in the bath after the fight with a bottle of champagne in his hands. 'Well, Jim,' he said with a wide grin, 'this sure puts the pressure on you.'

I made one mistake in my pre-fight preparation. After training to peak fitness with Terry in London, we returned to Glasgow a full week before the fight. It was too early. The city was like a furnace, burning with big fight talk and tension. I began to tighten up as the reality of how everybody was depending on me sank in. Too many people were considering me the champion before I had thrown a punch and I knew there was no way it was going to be that easy. Instead of feeding off the support I was in danger of allowing it to become a burden and again I started to worry about letting my followers down. All I wanted to do was clear my mind and concentrate exclusively on the fight, but there were a million distractions. It was the longest week of my life.

Terry and I had spent hours studying video film of Pitalua in action. He was a fighter who lacked finesse, but he tried to turn every punch he threw into a bomb and had plenty of resilience and strength. The Colombian had once been a street fighter and was a really tough hombre who had stopped nineteen of his thirty-four opponents inside the distance, mostly with hooks. He rarely threw a straight punch.

Our fight plan was to start cautiously and to keep Pitalua off balance and occupied with a procession of solid right jabs. We knew that he would be at his most dangerous in the early rounds and I was not to take any silly risks. I have often been criticized for being a slow starter, but in those first few rounds when I don't appear to be achieving much I am doing important exploratory work. I like to study my opponent and see what he has to offer before I reveal my full repertoire of punches. In fifteen-round fights I can afford the luxury of a full reconnaissance before opening up with my big guns. A fifteen-rounder is not a sprint. It's a marathon and I like to think I know just how to pace it.

The atmosphere in Kelvin Hall was just unbelievable. It was one giant Scottish celebration. There were flags and banners and football-style chants of 'Jim Watt . . . Jim Watt'. As I sat in the dressing-room in the last moments before going out into the arena, I could hear the unmistakable noise of bagpipes being warmed up ready for my entry into the ring.

Terry later gave a beautiful description of the effect the noise and tension being generated had on him. 'I felt as if a belt was being tightened around my chest,' he said. 'I've never known an atmosphere like it. It made what little hair I've got stand on end. Just think what it must have been doing to Pitalua and his handlers!'

There was muffled applause for Pitalua as he climbed into the ring. Terry, a battle-hardened pro, signalled to me to warm up and get a sweat on. It was nearly five minutes before I followed Pitalua into the ring and by then the crowd were at fever pitch. As I marched in behind the pipe band, I knew just what it must have been like to follow the bagpipes into battle. There is no more stirring sound in the world.

*

Deep, deep down I have always had the very private fear that when the pressure was really on me in the ring I would not have the courage to stand up to it. In boxing parlance, would I have the bottle to stick with it when the going got really tough? Any doubts I had were knocked away by Pitalua. I was so terrified of making a mess of it all that I failed to function properly in the early rounds. But I gradually came to terms with the enormous pressure and started to draw strength from the incredible support that was coming at me in great tidal waves of noise. My courage and conviction was severely tested in the fifth round when Pitalua landed the hardest punch I have ever taken. It was a swinging right hand to the side of the jaw and for a split second my legs didn't belong to me. At that instant I was as near to a knockout defeat as I have ever been in my career and it took enormous demands on my reserves of strength to stay on my feet and in the fight. In that most terrible moment I knew my hidden fears were unfounded. I had passed the test.

That was the turning point of the fight. Pitalua had hit me with his best shots and I was still there, scoring solidly with jabs and counterpunches. And I hadn't even started unloading my full, front-foot power.

Pitalua wanted that world title almost as badly as I did and he battled with every ounce of guts and energy in his body. But in the sixth round I started to really find my range and I had him gasping with thumping blows to the body. In round seven I caught him with a perfect left hook. As he fell to the canvas I mentally pleaded with him to stay down. 'Go on, be a sport and stay there,' I said to myself, but he was up and coming back at me after a count of eight.

I was getting mentally tired and feeling sorry for myself by the end of the tenth round. Pitalua was as brave and as strong as anybody I had ever met and I was beginning to get disheartened, seeing him still driving aggressively forward after I had hit him with my fiercest punches. It is at moments like these that 'nice guy' Terry Lawless deliberately turns nasty to motivate his boxers. He sensed that I needed a sharp reminder of what victory – and defeat – meant to me. 'If you're feeling tired, Jim, just think how the other feller feels,' he shouted, making himself heard above the din of the crowd. 'And remember, he hasn't got all these marvellous supporters on his side.'

He let that sink in and then added with real feeling: 'Just think what you and Margaret have taught little Michelle to say. "My daddy's the champion of the world." You can't let her down. And what about Andrew? You've promised to take the world championship belt home to him. Just think what victory means for Margaret and the kids. The title is there for the taking. Now go out and win it.'

In black and white, these words may not come across as being particularly inspiring. But they had the effect of a Churchillian speech on me and gave me that extra motivation I needed to put everything together for a victory effort.

In the twelfth round I *knew* I had at last got him. There comes a moment in a fight when, if you're lucky, you feel your opponent go. It's a look as much as anything that gives you the first indication. His eyes dull and he starts to look down rather than directly at you. Pitalua's eyes dulled as I pummelled him into the ropes in that twelfth round and as I unleashed a bombardment of punches, I realized he had nothing left to give in return.

The American referee, Arthur Mercante, pulled me away and I thought the championship was mine, but just as I was about to go into a jig he waved us back into action. I needed to call on all my years of experience to hold myself together and compose myself for a renewed onslaught at a time when my tired mind and body was pleading with me to switch off.

I sent Pitalua back into the ropes with a left-right combination and this time Mr Mercante, an excellent referee, acknowledged what I had sensed a minute before – that Pitalua had nothing left. He jumped in between us and raised my hand as the shattered but tremendously brave Colombian sagged back against the ropes. *I was the champion of the world.*

There was pandemonium as my arm went up. Terry and I cuddled like consenting adults. Everybody in the hall was up on their feet chanting and cheering and singing 'Flower of Scotland'. I had to suffer the terrible experience of being kissed by Mickey Duff. Then Margaret and my mother came

72

up on to the ring apron – as emotional a moment as I'll ever experience in my life. George Wiggs and Frank Black both gave me pats on the back and then, like the true pros they are, melted into the background to allow us Scots to get on with our celebrations. The Lord Provost looked as pleased as punch and wasn't even taken out of his stride when Terry, in a rare moment of total abandonment, kissed him on the cheek. 'Sorry about that,' Terry said with a grin, 'but you've done so much for us.'

'Don't worry,' the Provost said. 'The case will come up on Friday!'

Terry then slipped back into his usual role of Superpro. His main concern continued to be my welfare and he organized a police escort back to the dressing-room, where for the next hour he applied ice packs to my bumps and bruises. I had never before been so badly marked. It was without doubt the hardest, and most rewarding, fight of my life.

My hands were swollen and bruised and Terry, like a mother hen, warned anybody who came near me not to try to shake them. So they slapped me on the shoulders instead and by the time the night was out I was feeling as if I needed protective pads.

We had arranged to join the Lord Provost and the City Fathers in the Kelvin Hall banqueting room, but even with Hall Director Tom Malarkey's geographical knowledge to help us, we just couldn't get through the crowds of fans who seemed to be filling every corridor and doorway in the place. Mr Malarkey, whose assistance in making Kelvin Hall available was invaluable, finally conceded that it was a hopeless task and promised to give our apologies to the Lord Provost, David Hodge, and his colleagues to whom I shall always be indebted.

A small party of us slipped away for a quiet meal at a restaurant in the city centre. Maurice Hope and I sat facing each other across the table and that was really special for both of us. Like a couple of kids, we kept calling each other 'Champ'. I spent the rest of the night going from one celebration party to another. It seemed that nobody wanted to go to sleep and let the memorable night end. And that was also how it was for me, even though I had left all my strength and energy behind in the ring.

Everywhere I went people kept saying simply, 'Thank you.' It was as if I had returned something to them that they had lost. The pride was back in Scottish sport.

As I walked towards the Albany Hotel in the early hours of the morning to join another celebration party, a taxi screeched to a halt in the middle of the road. The driver jumped out and pushed a piece of paper in front of me. 'Let's have your autograph please, Jim,' he said. 'You've made us all feel like we're champions of the world.'

The last thing I had managed to do before leaving the dressing-room was relieve myself into a bottle so that the WBC officials could carry out the routine drug test.

'Isn't it marvellous,' I said to Terry. 'You become world champion and the first thing they want to do is take the piss out of you!'

At a crowded press conference the next day, or I should say later that day, Terry and I both vowed that my first defence of the championship would be in Glasgow. 'After the support I got last night there is no way I would go anywhere else in the world to defend it,' I said. And I meant it.

My darling Michelle stole the show at the conference. I think she kissed just about everybody in the place and kept repeating over and over again: 'My daddy's champion of the world.' One day when she's old enough to understand I shall tell her how a reminder of those words at the end of the tenth round helped me win the title.

Round 9

The Apprenticeship

It had taken me sixteen years to become an overnight star. I served a long and demanding apprenticeship before I became world champion and as I look back to the Jim Watt I used to be, I realize how easily I could have become a non-starter.

The reputation of being a fighter appealed to me more than the actual fighting in the early days. Aggression is a way of life in Glasgow and I liked people to know I was useful with my fists. But it was all for show. Deep down I wasn't completely hooked on boxing. Most of all, I didn't like the fear that comes before a fight. It was more wearing than the training or the boxing. I was a bit like a flashy gunfighter, cockily showing off the six-shooters on his hip, but not too concerned if he wasn't called on to use them. I could always fantasize a great fight. When I was a kid, I remember how I used to stand in front of a mirror at home, with a crust of bread in my mouth as a make-believe gumshield, and knocked out all my imaginary opponents with crashing combination punches. Jim Watt, the looking-glass champ.

My appetite and keenness for boxing started to change as Jim Murray got through to me with his training techniques and driving enthusiasm. He lived and breathed boxing and his fanaticism gradually rubbed off on me. It was almost auto-suggestion as he fed ideas and theories to me for hours on end, filling my head with stories of the old-time fighters like Benny Lynch, Tancy Lee, Jimmy Wilde, Jackie Paterson, Jackie Brown and Peter Kane. I listened and learned. He hit me with such a torrent of words that it's a wonder I haven't got a cauliflower ear.

75

His eyes blazing with passion, Murray used to take me for atmosphere-soaking walks along Florence Street on Glasgow's south side.

'This is where Benny Lynch used to live when he was your age,' he would explain. 'Can't you feel the magic in the air? He used to walk up this very street dreaming of one day conquering the world with his fists. And his dream came true.'

The magic *did* rub off on me and I *did* start dreaming of conquering the world. I was just fifteen, an apprentice electrician, and already I was setting my sights on one day fighting as a professional. Jim Murray nurtured this dream. He was one of the few amateur trainers who also held a professional manager's licence and there was soon an unwritten agreement that one day we would be partners in the pro game.

Mind you, nearly all my dreams seemed wrecked in my fifth amateur contest when I suffered my first defeat. A boxer called Harrison from Coupar took my breath away with a punch to the solar plexus. I went down like a punctured balloon and when I got up the referee decided I was in no condition to continue. It was then that I realized the thing I hated most of all in life was losing. Jim Murray had to be at his most persuasive to convince me that it was worth continuing with my career.

The contest that gave me a nationwide reputation was against John Stracey in the 1968 ABA semifinals at Manchester. Stracey was the seventeen-year-old boxer everybody was talking about. He had beaten the almost legendary Terry Waller in the London finals and I qualified to meet him by winning the Scottish lightweight title and then my quarter-final against Howard Hayes.

I have BBC TV commentator Harry Carpenter to thank for my victory over Hayes. Hayes had been knocking all his opponents over with what Jim Murray and I had heard was a vicious right-hand punch and all our concentration in training was on me avoiding right hands, moving to my right and keeping my left up guarding my chin. Harry came into our dressing-room before the contest to get some biographical details and just happened to mention in casual conversation that Hayes was doing all the damage with a *left* hook. This meant a hurried change of tactics and although Hayes shook me to my boots with a left hook in the first round, I recovered to beat him on points and therefore clinch a place in the semifinals.

Murray and I closely studied Stracey's startling performance against Waller on television. We noted that he rarely threw a straight punch and liked to curve all his shots. In the month leading up to the semifinals we worked non-stop in training to make certain that my punches were straight and short.

Our strategy would be to wait for Stracey to send his punches travelling in an arc and then counter with short, straight blows through what would be a wide-open defence.

When I arrived at Manchester for the contest, I saw a lad who I took to be Stracey's younger brother. I couldn't believe it when somebody pointed him out as being my opponent. It was my first view of him in the flesh and I couldn't help thinking he looked like a boy on a man's errand. He never did lose that baby-face look.

Stracey came bouncing out to meet me in the centre of the ring before the first bell and as we touched gloves I clearly recall him saying in a Cockney accent: 'Right, cock, let's go.'

Thirty-five seconds later it was all over. Stracey pulled back his left ready to throw one of his roundhouse punches and I fired a short right cross flush to his jaw. His eyes crossed and he crashed backwards with no hope in the world of beating the ten-second count. To this day I don't think I've ever hit anybody harder or with sweeter timing.

That defeat left a deep scar on Stracey and an even deeper one on his father, who never kept it a secret that he was his son's number one fan. He always talked a great fight on behalf of John, for whom I had enormous admiration as an outstanding fighter.

Years later when we were stablemates in the Terry Lawless camp, his father was watching me spar and announced to the rest of the gymnasium: 'Watch him, he punches with his eyes closed. They were closed the night he got lucky and knocked my John out.'

I picked my moment for a counterpunch. 'The last time I

had my eyes shut was when you had your mouth shut,' I said with a spite that often comes to my tongue when I am getting keyed up for an approaching fight.

Mr Stracey and I never again exchanged words. But it has not lessened my rating of his son as a fighter. At his peak under Terry Lawless he was magnificent.

Millions of BBC Television viewers saw me flatten him in one round and suddenly I was being talked of as a gold medal prospect for the 1968 Olympics in Mexico. But I had other ideas.

Baron de Coubertin would have been disgusted with my decision not to box for Britain in the 1968 Olympic Games in Mexico. He was the French gentleman who founded the modern Olympics and laid down the creed, 'The important thing is not to win but to take part.' That does not capture my sporting philosophy. For me, winning is everything. It is only by being completely single-minded about winning that I have managed to get to the top of my profession.

I won the ABA lightweight title in 1968 and automatically qualified for the British Olympic team. There was a huge outcry when I declined to take part. Jim Murray and I agreed that publicly my reason would be that I was having problems making the 9 st 7 lb weight, which was perfectly true. I had been on a starvation diet in the week leading up to the ABA final and boxed without sparkle on my way to a points victory against Bobby Fisher. But even without the weight worry, there was no way I wanted to go to the Olympics as just another competitor. I was realistic enough to appreciate that after just thirty-seven amateur contests, thirteen of them in the youth section, I was still a virtual novice in Olympic terms. In Mexico there would be battle-hardened Americans, Russians and Eastern Europeans who would have had four times as many contests.

There was also the problem of boxing at high altitude to be taken into account and after careful consideration I decided that I would give the Olympics a miss. I would have loved to have gone out there and represented my country with pride, but feared being shamed. The gold medal was, I knew, out of my reach at that stage of my career and nothing else interested me.

I got a roasting from the selectors. One of them went so far as to say: 'We are very annoyed and distressed. He has let us down badly.' However, he was not having to get into the ring to do the boxing and I was annoyed and distressed by his reaction.

Baron de Coubertin's creed of taking part being more important than winning might be all right for athletes, swimmers and competitors in sports that don't involve physical contact. But a boxer who gets into the ring with anything less than total commitment can get seriously hurt.

Anyway, John Stracey took my place in the Olympic team and came home empty-handed after being beaten by eventual champion Ronnie Harris, who a few years later gave Alan Minter a rare defeat in the professional ring.

I could so easily have got knocked about as an amateur if it had not been for the caring and conscientious way in which Jim Murray handled me. He pulled me out of Scottish international matches against Russia and Rumania because he knew I did not have sufficient experience to compete at that level against Iron Curtain boxers who were professional in everything but name.

I will always be grateful to Jim Murray for handling me with care at this vital learning stage in my career. Now we were ready for the challenge of professional boxing.

I was paid £60 for my professional debut at Hamilton Town Hall on 30 October 1968. As an £18-a-week apprentice electrician, I was delighted with the pay day. My big ambition at the time was one day to earn £500 for a fight. That I thought would be proof that I had really made the grade.

The cynics who said that I had fabricated the story about not being able to make the 9 st 7 lb limit for the Olympics were silenced by the fact that I made my debut in the light-welterweight division. I weighed in at 9 st 11½ lb. My opponent, Santos Martins of Ghana, tipped the scales at 10 st.

My mother and sister, Jean, reluctantly came to see me fight for the first time. Both had given me all the encouragement and support that I could have asked for at home but neither had been able to face actually seeing me get into the ring. Even now Jean hates watching me fight and says she feels the punches more than I do. My wife Margaret is always at the ringside and her presence has a calming influence on me. I leave her to do the worrying for me.

On the night I made my debut I was scheduled to be second on the programme and passed this information on to Mum and Jean. The contestants for the first fight were held up and at the last minute I was switched to opening spot on the bill. Mum and Jean watched Santos Martins climb into the ring, unaware that he was my opponent. He had a superb physique with wide shoulders and spectacular muscles. Jean turned to Mum and said: 'Och, some poor wee boy is going to be in for it.'

Then I appeared. A bottle of milk with gloves on. Jean ran out of the hall feeling terrified for me and was not around to see me pummel Martins to a fourth-round knockout defeat.

I don't exactly petrify opponents with my appearance. I am so slim that I have to jump around in the shower to get wet and my skin is so pale that you would think I had just been the distance with Dracula. When I sit in the sun I don't tan. I don't even burn. I stroke. But this undernourished look does have its advantages. Opponents look at me and tend to get overconfident. I have yet to see a Mr Universe win a world boxing title. Overdeveloped muscles slow a boxer down and add nothing to his punching power. It is the timing of the punches that matters as much as the weight of them.

I was so full of nerves the night I made by debut that I have only hazy memories of what happened. All I wanted was to get the fight over and done with. It is only now that I look back that I feel sorry for Martins. I climbed into the ring with a lot of local support and full of hope and ambition. He was all alone in the hall and had come up to Glasgow from London just for a £50 pay day. His homeland of Ghana must have seemed a million miles away.

After I had got over my initial nerves, I unleashed my first

sustained attack in the fourth round and he quickly surrendered. I caught him with a left hook to the jaw and he took
the full count while resting on one knee.

I was back at Hamilton Town Hall again two months later
for my second fight. This time I felt more assured and
confident and I stopped Alex Gibson of Belfast in the second
round. I again did the damage with a left hook and remember
him folding slowly to the canvas as if in an action-replay
sequence.

Ken Buchanan, then British lightweight champion, topped
the bill promoted by Sammy Docherty. I barely knew Buchanan, but was to have my name linked with his so often over
the next five years that I was to get totally sick of him.

After just two fights, Jim Murray started bracketing me
with Buchanan. He told Jimmy Sanderson, then of the *Scottish
Daily Express*: 'Our aim is to build Jim Watt up as a challenger
to Ken Buchanan for the British lightweight title. Watt can
pull in the crowds because of his devastating punching and I
have refused good offers from England so that Scotland can
see him.'

This was Murray banging the promotional drum. He had
gone into partnership with promoter John Ness, and I topped
their first bill at Govan Town Hall in Glasgow on 10 April
1969. The seat prices ranged from five bob to thirty shillings
and I got something like £80 for my third professional fight.
This do-it-yourself approach by Jim Murray was the only way
he could guarantee getting me fights in Scotland, where the
professional scene was about as lively as a graveyard.

My opponent was Victor Paul, who had been lined up for
my debut and again for my second contest but had called off
each time. I wish he hadn't turned up at the third time of
asking. The fight had a lasting psychological effect on me.
Paul was nicknamed the 'Iron Man' by the press and before
the fight boasted: 'No one can put me down.' At the final bell,
I was inclined to believe him.

It had been four months since my previous contest and I
lacked sharpness. But after three rounds I had got into my
stride and I was finding Paul so easy to hit that I was
confident I could stop him inside the scheduled eight rounds.

In rounds four, five and six, I hit him with everything but the corner stool and he was still standing and occasionally dangerous with swinging haymaker punches. I boxed through the last two rounds virtually by instinct. I had punched myself to the edge of exhaustion and at the end, having won all eight rounds, I didn't have the strength to blow out a candle.

From that night on I decided I would pace myself in the early rounds so that I could conserve my energy for distance fights and I started to get a reputation as a slow starter. Victor Paul was to blame and I had two more helpings of him to come.

This fight had generated a thought in my mind that perhaps I lacked stamina. It was certainly nothing to do with a lack of proper preparation. I was running through Ruchill Park every morning at 7 a.m., always finishing a four-mile work-out with 'chin up' exercises on the swing supports in the children's playground. Then I would have a special milk and fruit breakfast before going to work as an electrician with the James Scott Company. I started each evening programme with half an hour of Yoga exercises to develop natural relaxation, deep concentration and breath control. After a tea of more health foods prescribed by Jim Murray, I would join him at the gymnasium for a ninety-minute schedule of explosive exercises, bag punching, sparring and technique training.

It was five months before I was back in the ring, this time against experienced Jamaican Winston Thomas. I wore him down with a volley of punches in the opening minute of the eighth and last round, and referee Benny Caplan stopped it after I had trapped Thomas in a neutral corner with no escape from the hail of leather I was sending his way.

This was my first professional fight in London and my first experience of boxing in front of a sporting-club audience. Jack Solomons was the promoter of the show at the World Sporting Club, which is based in the Grosvenor Hotel in Mayfair. I was concentrating so hard on trying to win in style that I was unable to gauge the atmosphere, but I can now state after more than a dozen fights in clubs that I much prefer boxing on commercial shows where there is an atmosphere that sets the competitive juices running. It's harder to get motivated in an elegant club setting with everybody attired in dinner jackets.

Boxing News stated that at that stage of my career I bore comparison with another southpaw, the great Dave Charnley. I considered it a real tribute. Charnley had been British and European lightweight champion and had given one of the all-time greats, Joe Brown, a lot of trouble in two world title fights. He was winding down his career in my first year as an amateur and I studied films of his superb counterpunching style. Walter McGowan, who has since become a good friend, was another inspiration for me. He proved a Scot could battle through to the top by winning the world flyweight championship in 1966.

Jim Murray had now despaired of getting boxing off its knees in Glasgow. He had dreams of becoming the Solomons or Harry Levene of Scotland, but there were neither the fighters nor the public interest to match his ambitions. I became almost a permanent fixture on private club shows and I was about as well known to the general sporting public as an extra in a Hollywood B-movie.

Fight number five was at the famous National Sporting Club which has its headquarters at the Café Royal in London's Piccadilly. In the opposite corner was that cunning old pro Tommy Tiger who was having his 111th and final contest. He had started boxing in his native Nigeria in the 1950s, when I was still in junior school, and while he didn't win more than half of his contests, he was always a handful for opponents with his bustling style. I was worried at one stage in the fight that Tommy was going to finish his long career with a victory. From the third round on I boxed virtually one-handed after damaging knuckles on my left fist when misconnecting with a hook against Tiger's iron-hard head. Jim Murray was anxious at the end of the round when I told him what had happened and suggested I should see how I coped with keeping Tommy on the end of a right jab. At the end of the fourth I told Jim that everything was all right and I managed to win comfortably on points without letting on to Tiger that I was badly handicapped.

Throughout my career, amateur and professional, I have suffered from bruised hands and jarred wrists. It is something I have learned to live with and there have often been times in the ring when punching an opponent has hurt me more than them. But I pride myself on never letting the man in the other corner know if and when I am in pain. That would give him hope, and hope is what you attempt to hammer out of the opposition. As I have said, boxing is as much psychological as physical and I always set out to be stronger minded than my opponents. Both Jim Murray and, later, Terry Lawless encouraged me to box with my brain as well as my fists. For me, it is still the Noble Art.

Because of my hand injury, it was three months before I was able to box again. I was scheduled to meet Jackie Lee, a southpaw from Hoxton, but at the last moment National Sporting Club matchmaker Les Roberts found me a substitute, Victor Paul. I was getting around £150 and knew I was going to have to earn it.

Jim Murray missed this fight because his mother was ill. My cousin, Bert Watt, an experienced amateur trainer, was in my corner and everything was going to plan when a tiring Paul caught me with a butt in the closing seconds of the sixth round. Suddenly I had a curtain of blood blurring the vision in my right eye and referee Sid Nathan acted swiftly to stop the fight. I was desperately disappointed but Mr Nathan did me a favour because one blow on the gash could have caused serious damage. When I inspected the injury in the dressing-room mirror after the fight I could see that it was in a nasty position, just to the right of my right eyebrow. It was star shaped and deep enough to keep pumping blood. The Board of Control doctor came to the dressing-room with his little black bag and I sat biting my tongue while he got to work with his sewing kit. The thought of being stitched is much worse than the actual stitching. The doctor expertly did his needle-work for about six minutes and closed the wound with five stitches. I have the scar today to remind me of my first bitter taste of defeat as a pro.

Four months later I was back in the ring for a 'rubber' match with Victor Paul and I thought I was doomed to another defeat when he caught me with a sickening head butt in the first round. Jim Murray worked on a cut on my left eyebrow during the break and warned me to keep the fight at long distance and not get involved in a brawl. But the fight turned my way in the second round when I dropped him for two counts. It was a tremendous psychological boost for me because Paul had boasted that nobody could put him off his feet and I had started to believe it. When I saw him on the canvas I knew he was there for the taking and by the fifth round I had pummelled him with so many punches that referee Harry Gibbs had to step in to stop what had become a farcically onesided fight. Victor Paul. What a brave lion of a man. My eyebrows bleed at the mention of his name!

The latest eye injury was not serious enough to stop me taking another fight date two weeks later at the Great International Sporting Club in Nottingham, this time against Welsh lightweight champion Bryn Lewis. Poor Bryn was made for my counterpunching style and I don't think I missed him throughout six one-sided rounds before the referee wisely rescued him after I had continually driven him to the ropes.

After the summer close season I was looking forward to stepping up my activity and earning power. My highest wage to date had been £200 for the third fight against Paul at the National Sporting Club. I was hardly getting rich and was continuing to combine boxing with my work as an electrician. Much of my work was done on the trade stands at Kelvin Hall, which later in my career was to become a hall of fame for me. There was a slow spell when I was forced to go on the dole but I found the personal questions I was asked so humiliating that I just couldn't bring myself to make regular visits to the social services office. It was 29 October 1970 before I got another fight and I had to go to Ireland for it.

I was astonished by the warmth of my welcome when I got into the Ulster Hall ring to meet Lisburn southpaw Sammy Lockhart. The cheers were so loud when I was introduced that I thought I was boxing back home in Glasgow. It was only later that I was told all the Catholics in the audience were on my side and willing me to beat Lockhart, who was a Protestant. The fact that I was also a Protestant didn't matter to them!

During the summer I had been working at perfecting my body punches and the practice paid off in style. I almost cut

Sammy in half with a right hook to the solar plexus and he went down as if he had been stabbed. The fight was into the middle of the second round and we had been firing punches at each other as if it were the start of a war. We had both been stoked up by the electric atmosphere in the hall. It had made such a difference to me after so long fighting behind closed doors in private clubs. Sammy pulled himself up at eight, but was obviously still winded and I immediately fired another punch to the body, this time a long left. He went down on his hands and knees fighting for breath while the referee counted the ten seconds, each one cheered by the Catholics in the crowd. The fervour of the spectators stayed as a deep memory and I was to have reason to recall it at a later date in my career when pressure was being put on me to go to Derry to fight Charlie Nash.

After this emphatic win, Jim Murray issued the first positive challenge to Ken Buchanan, who was now recognized in some quarters as lightweight champion of the world as well as Great Britain.

'He should either fight Watt or relinquish the British title and concentrate on his world championship affairs,' Murray said. 'Give the young contenders in the lightweight division a chance. We're prepared to consider meeting Buchanan in a non-title fight over eight rounds, provided the money is right. It would fill any hall in Scotland.'

But Buchanan, as I'm sure Murray guessed he would, turned a deaf ear to the challenge. Even though I was already rated No. 2 contender for the British title, it was clearly too early for me to get into the ring with such an experienced opponent.

I had just completed two years as a professional, during which I'd had only nine contests and three of those were against the same opponent, Victor Paul. Murray was having nightmares trying to get me matches that were acceptable.

'The worst thing you ever did was knocking out John Stracey in one round,' he said once. 'It has frightened all the opposition away.'

People in the game were soon whispering Murray in the back, coming up to me when he wasn't around and saying that he was the wrong manager for me. 'You should go down south to London where the action is,' they would urge. 'Murray hasn't got the right connections. He's a nobody in professional boxing.'

It was pointed out that John Stracey had turned professional with Terry Lawless eleven months after me and yet within a year had fought eleven times. Like me, Stracey made his pro debut against Santos Martins and knocked him out in two rounds.

In a desperate bid to get me some action, Murray issued a challenge through *Boxing News* to Stracey. But John had a shrewd manager who didn't want to know me as an opponent.

It suited me to go along at the pace Jim Murray was setting for me, but I was beginning to itch for some of the big money that other fighters were supposed to be earning. The whisperers said that the likes of Stracey would never get into the ring for less than a thousand pounds. I had yet to earn half that for a fight.

In fairness to Murray, I should point out that he could have got me a lot more fights if he had agreed to put me in out of my depth. But he wanted to bring me along carefully and refused to let me be used as a 'fodder' fighter against more experienced opponents.

In retrospect I can now fully understand why top-line promoters like Harry Levene, Mike Barrett and Mickey Duff did not want to use me on their major shows. Down in London I was a virtual unknown. Commercial shows are run for profit rather than prestige and in the early days of my career I would, as Mickey Duff puts it, have taken only my bag with me to a London venue. There would have been no supporters. The promoters, quite understandably, gave first call to London-based boxers who could sell tickets. Even when I topped a Royal Albert Hall bill as late as 1976 I recall the *Daily Mail* referring to me in a headline as 'Jim Who?' And I was British champion at the time.

I went back into the clubs to beat Ron Clifford of Pudsey – he retired at the end of the fourth with a hand injury – and the French title contender David Presenti, a late substitute whom I beat comfortably on points.

Then, on 22 March 1971 I produced my best performance to date in what was scheduled to be my first ten-round contest at the National Sporting Club against the highly rated Frenchman Henri Nesi. I was apprehensive about going the full distance and made my customary cautious start to conserve energy. But when I opened up in the third round I realized that Nesi would fold under pressure. Nesi had nothing to offer in the sixth after I had pinned him against the ropes under a heavy barrage of punches and I was relieved when referee Harry Gibbs stopped it because I could have seriously hurt him. Film of the fight was shown on BBC's Grandstand the following Saturday afternoon and at last people outside clubland began to realize I existed.

Murray stepped up his campaign to get Buchanan either to defend the British title or relinquish it. He had become undisputed world champion the previous month and it was obvious that he had no intention of putting the British title on the line. I considered his attitude selfish in the extreme. The British Boxing Board of Control refused to take any notice of newspaper talk that Buchanan was ready to give up the championship and they nominated Willie Reilly and me to meet in a final eliminator. At last, I was to box on a major London show.

Round 10

The Short-Notice Champion

Harry Levene, who has been in the game so long that he is the patriarch of promoters, staged my eliminator with Willy Reilly at Wembley Arena as a support to the triple heavyweight championship contest between Joe Bugner and Jack Bodell. I was to be paid my highest purse to date: £600. It was my thirteenth professional fight and I had realized my ambition of earning more than £500 for a night's work.

I had boxed at Wembley only once before, when I won the ABA lightweight title in 1968. It is a large, impersonal place and after my succession of fights in hotel banqueting suites, it was like going into an aircraft hangar to box. Most of the crowd had come only to see the heavyweight battle and the place was not exactly humming with anticipation when Reilly and I climbed into the ring.

There was quite a lot of support for Reilly, who was based at Wembley after moving south from Scotland, where he had started his career under Jim Murray's management. Jim knew Reilly's style and character well and we had a careful plan of campaign mapped out. I really wanted to impress the London fans but could not have had a more frustrating opponent than Reilly, who was a wily, spoiling craftsman who could have made Racquel Welch look bad. We did little to bring spectators to the edge of their seats before I opened a gash over Willie's left eye with a right hook in the seventh round and referee Harry Gibbs stopped the fight. It was not the stylish way in which I had dreamt of winning and the knowledgeable Wembley audience was totally underwhelmed by my performance.

Anyway, I was now the official challenger for Ken Buchanan's British championship, but I knew I had more chance of getting into the ring with Jack Buchanan. It was obvious that there was no way he would defend his British crown against me while he was world champion. I didn't blame Ken for wanting to cash in on his world title, but, in fairness to all hungry British contenders, he should have relinquished the domestic championship months before.

While waiting for Buchanan to make up his mind, I topped a charity show at the National Sporting Club in aid of the King George VI's Fund for Sailors. Prince Philip was at the ringside and I was anxious to please. Once again I had a substitute thrown at me at the last minute and what a classy opponent they came up with. I was matched over ten rounds with ex-French champion, Leonard Tavarez, who had boxed in the highest company and had twice taken Buchanan the distance.

Tavarez, born in Senegal, had been stopped only once in a long career and that because of a damaged eye. I contented myself with piling up the points with stiff jabs, keeping the fight at long distance after I had broken from a clinch in the second round with blood seeping from a cut over my left eye. The wound gradually worsened and I sensed that referee Harry Gibbs was considering halting the fight after he came to my corner to inspect the injury at the end of the seventh and eighth rounds. I went into the ninth round determined to stop Tavarez before he could inflict any more damage to the eye and had him staggering under an all-out attack when the ref rescued him. It was probably the best win of my career to date and I began to think that perhaps Buchanan was not too big a mountain to climb.

At last there was positive news from Buchanan and, sure enough, he decided to relinquish his British title rather than defend it against me and also put at risk his world championship. Willie Reilly and I were ordered back into the ring again, this time with the British title as the prize for the winner.

The fight, staged at the Nottingham Ice Rink on 1 February 1972, deteriorated into one of the saddest occasions of my life. I had set my heart on winning the championship and was jabbing my way to victory when Willie caught me with his head in the last moments of the seventh round. You don't *feel* yourself cut and the first evidence you have is when you sense a warm trickle on your face. But this time I was in no doubt that the injury was a bad one because the blood was gushing from a deep wound over my right eye. Referee Roland Dakin twice inspected the injury before finally stopping the fight in the tenth round after a left hook from Reilly had made the blood flow again. 'Sorry, Jim,' the ref said as he led me back to the corner where Jim Murray was looking like a corpse. 'I just can't let you risk any further damage.' The injury required seven stitches.

I wept tears of frustration in the shower after the fight. The British title was the goal I had set myself and now it seemed a million miles away. This was the fourth time I had received a nasty cut over one of my eyes and I wondered about the point of going on with my career if I was going to be continually let down by weak flesh. I knew in my heart I was a more accomplished fighter than Reilly and I sensed that he knew it too. I was certain that he would not want to defend the championship against me, so I was at a complete standstill. After more than three years as a professional I was a nowhere man. Jim Who?

This mood of despondency was still with me and I couldn't find the will power to resume training when, three months later, I suddenly got my ambitions and hopes switched back on. Reilly had been ordered to defend his championship against Coventry challenger Tony Riley at Solihull's Midlands Sporting Club. Just eight days before the fight Willie astonished everybody by announcing that he would rather retire than fight for a £1806 share of the purse money.

Jim Murray contacted me and asked if I would take the fight at such short notice. I had done no preparation work whatsoever, but to me this was a chance in a million and I jumped at it. Reilly's sudden decision to surrender the title after he had worked so hard to win it completely baffled me. I would have fought for the championship for nothing. First of all there was the honour of being British champion and, secondly, I could see the title as a passport to greater things.

We agreed to take the fight with Riley for the vacant title on a 60–40 basis, the winner to take the lion's share of the £3010 purse. It meant that, win or lose, I would be having my biggest pay day.

Jim Murray and I did not know a lot about Tony Riley, but an article in *Boxing News* quoted him as saying that he had sometimes lacked dedication and he admitted once having been on a drinking spree when his bodyweight ballooned up above 12 stone. Even with eight days' notice, I quietly fancied my chances of winning.

Few boxers could have got into the ring with less training behind them than I had for that title fight. I sparred only twelve rounds and my fitness work was only a tenth of what it would normally have been for a fifteen-round fight. Yet right from the first bell I was charged up with super confidence because I was convinced I could outgun Riley. For the first time in my career I had to go more than ten rounds, but I paced myself cautiously and was always in command with right jabs that continually speared through Riley's guard. He was cut and swollen around his left eye and I was just softening him up for the kill when referee Harry Gibbs stepped in to hold my arm aloft with four seconds of the twelfth round to go.

I was champion of Great Britain and had earned my top pay packet of £1806. When the Lonsdale Belt was fastened around my waist at the end, I vowed that I would win it outright. I am one of those people who always needs a target in life. The British title had been my Everest. Now I needed to shift my sights higher.

But my thoughts that the championship would lead me into an Aladdin's Cave were slowly stifled. I was still not wanted on the big commercial shows and it was at this stage in my career that I began to wonder if Jim Murray had the necessary push to open the right doors for me. I had to wait seven months for my first fight as British champion and I was back behind the closed doors of the National Sporting Club where I stopped Noel McIvor, the Southern Area champion from Luton, with a cut eye in three rounds of a non-title fight.

Meantime Ken Buchanan, who had lost his world light-

weight title in a controversial battle with the now legendary
Roberto Duran, was back hunting for the British crown, and
we were at last to get together in the same ring on the opening
night of the St Andrew's Sporting Club at Glasgow's Albany
Hotel.

Buchanan and Me

I felt like Jim Murray's hit man when I went into the ring to defend the British championship against Ken Buchanan at about 11.15 p.m. on the evening of 29 January 1973. For nearly two years Murray had been hurling insults and challenges at Buchanan in a bid to get me a lucrative fight date. It had started out as a purely business venture, but Jim could never do anything by halves. He began to believe the things he was saying about Buchanan and became almost paranoid about him.

It all got nasty and personal when Buchanan went on television and described Murray as the worst manager in Britain and me as nothing better than a two-round job who didn't belong in the same ring as him. He then watched my fight against Noel McIvor and commented: 'It is the first time I have ever seen him in action and he is even worse than I thought. If he fights like that against me, then it won't last long.'

It was an unnecessary insult from Buchanan and it convinced me he was more concerned about me than he cared to admit. He certainly didn't say it to sell tickets because our championship contest had been signed for a private club. Since my title win, he had lost his world crown to the devastating Duran and he was clearly worried that a defeat by 'Jim Who?' would wipe out any chance of a world championship return. He was trying to put psychological pressure on me, but Murray was more than a match for him in the verbal stakes and had become totally obsessed with the fight.

Murray hit back with such jewels as: 'I want this to be a fight where one or the other will be carried out of the ring. I know it won't be Jim Watt. . . . Buchanan is a light puncher and it makes me laugh when I hear him say that he'll annihilate Jim. I have gone over his record with a magnifying glass and have come to the conclusion that he couldn't annihilate a mouse. . . .'

Looking back, I wonder if it would have been a better contest if Buchanan and Murray had fought! They had a genuine dislike for each other that went beyond the sort of gimmicks that are drummed up for selling tickets.

I have to admit that Buchanan is not my favourite person, but I respect him as a fighter. I thought he was selfish the way he clung on to the British title when he was world champion, so stopping the young boxers down the scale from progressing and earning money. He had no intention of defending the British crown and should have relinquished it at least a year before he finally let it go.

As a boxer he was a skilled craftsman and I admired the way he went into hostile territory all over the world and time and again came away the winner against top-flight opponents. I thought he might have been an even better fighter had he slowed down a litttle. At his peak, he moved so fast that he could never settle himself to land really heavy blows.

The Buchanan fight came a year too early for me. Terry Lawless has since told me that he thinks it was unwise to put me in the ring with him at that stage of my career. It was not as if we were earning a fortune. As champion I was collecting £4200. Ken's 40 per cent share of the purse was £2400. It was my best pay day but it was not a massive sum when you think of what we could have earned with a well-promoted commercial show.

It was the seventeenth fight of my professional career and I was still a novice by Buchanan's standards. He had fought forty-seven times and been beaten only twice, including the disputed loss of his title to Duran. Like me, Ken had suffered from being hidden from the public for too long on club shows and because he could never attract big audiences in Britain he adopted a 'have-gloves-will-travel' policy that took him to all corners of the globe. Compared to him, I was still a learner.

Peter Keenan, an outstanding Glasgow bantamweight of the

1950s and still an influential figure in Scottish boxing, added extra venom to our fight when he came out strongly on my side and said of Buchanan: 'He is all mouth. I will bet Buchanan £1000 that he cannot correctly name the round in which he will beat Watt and I will bet him a further £1,000 that if anyone is knocked out it will be him and not Watt.' As Peter said that he would give his winnings to the Drumchapel Sports Centre, everybody in Glasgow naturally applauded his outspoken views. But in Buchanan's home town of Edinburgh the Keenan challenge was greeted with sneers of contempt and it crowded more pressure on Buchanan and me before a punch had been thrown.

Our fight was an out-and-out war. Once again I was handicapped by a cut right eyebrow which started bleeding in the second round, but Danny Holland, Henry Cooper's former 'cuts man', had been hired for the night and did an excellent job keeping the injury in check. Buchanan went up in my estimation. Several times during the fight I could feel him fading as I scored with barrages of combination punches, but he showed tremendous character and courage and each time called on hidden reserves to haul himself back into the fight.

I lost the contest and the championship in the last two rounds. It was unchartered territory as far as I was concerned and I found the fourteenth and fifteenth rounds tough going, while Buchanan fell back on his vast experience to score with crisper and sharper punches. Many people at the ringside thought I had just about done enough to win, but the decision of Edinburgh referee George Smith went to the man from Edinburgh. I could not argue with the verdict and felt Buchanan deserved it. But I had given him the fright and the fight of his life. As we hugged each other at the end of a bitterly fought battle, he said he bore no grudge against me.

Buchanan tried to make his peace with Jim Murray, but my manager was eaten up with bitterness and refused to shake his hand. There was an intensity about Murray's hatred that made me wonder about our future together. He had a chip on his shoulder the size of an oak tree and his black moods were beginning to make me feel edgy.

This is the victory that gave me the most satisfying moment of my amateur career. That's John Stracey just coming round after being knocked out in forty-five seconds of our ABA semifinal in 1968

Jim Murray, my first manager and an influential man in my life, points me in the right direction

Ken Buchanan's face is in the middle of a leather sandwich as I land a right jab in our 1973 British title fight. Ken was a points winner but I gave almost as good as I got in what was only the seventeenth fight of my career

Opposite. A master at work. This is a superb study of Terry Lawless going about his business in the corner, with trainer Frank Black in support. With George Wiggs, they form the best corner team in boxing

I have just become European champion in eighty-two seconds against André Holyk and the Frenchman is inconsolable. At this moment I needed a quick French translation for "Sorry mate. . . ."

Referee Wally Thom counts and it adds up to misery for my fellow-Scot Johnny Cheshire. I stopped the brave Ayrshire man in seven rounds to retain my British title

Terry Lawless swears he could see my world champion stablemate
Maurice Hope by looking through my ear. Super Mo and I are the
best of buddies in and out of the gymnasium. We are always at the
ringside to support each other

Alfredo Pitalua's victory sign before our world title fight proved
premature and wrong. Promoter partners Mike Barrett and Mickey Duff
are in the background. I owe them both a vote of thanks for projecting
me in front of my fellow Scots

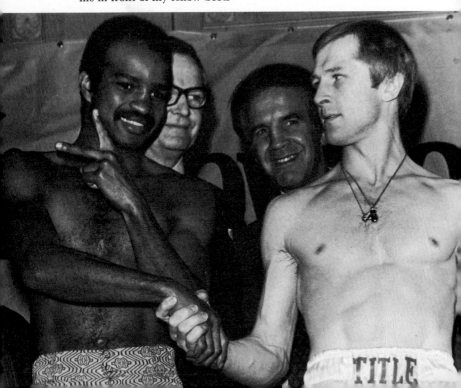

The sweetest moment of my life. I have just become champion of the world as referee Arthur Mercante signals that Pitalua has taken enough punishment in round 12 of an unforgettable title fight

The two Mrs Watts in my life. Mum and my wife, Margaret, climbed into the ring to join in the victory celebrations after I had become lightweight champion of the world

The pressure on Margaret when she watches me fight is immense and she often bolts from the ringside if the going gets tough for me. But the world championship trophy (bottom right) makes it all worthwhile

Four very good reasons why I carry on fighting. I want to make the future secure for Margaret, Andrew, Michelle and Jim Junior, who is in Margaret's arms. The picture of me in the background is the only time I enjoyed being put on the canvas

I am a great admirer of Henry Cooper. He represents our sport with dignity, a behaviour pattern I gladly copy

BBC's voice of boxing, Harry Carpenter. His attention to detail helped me win a vital contest during my amateur career (see Round 9)

The Lord Provost, David Hodge, has just announced that my world title fight against Pitalua belongs to Glasgow. The Provost is the No. 1 man in Scotland in my book

Would you buy a second-hand car from either of these men? This is me getting publicity for my car showroom with my business partner and right-hand man, Arthur Morrison

A weight off my mind. I have
just scaled bang on 9 st 9 lbs for
my world title defence against
Roberto Vasquez. I take great pride
in controlling my weight to within
ounces of the lightweight limit

By the left . . . this is typical
of the punches with which I
vanquished Vasquez

Have I got news for you! Mickey Duff, my most unforgettable
character, is about to ask me what sort of razor I use!

It's the final blow for Charlie Nash (*above*) as referee Sid Nathan intervenes. Terry Lawless and I find the Glasgow atmosphere very embracing (*below*) after I have won The World title. A fan joins in!

Before the Davis fight . . .

During the Davis fight . . .

After the Davis fight . . .

'Flower of Scotland' . . .

Round 9 against O'Grady, and I'm in trouble with a cut right eye . . .

Round 10 against O'Grady, and the American is cut on the forehead . . .

O'Grady sportingly acknowledges me as the winner and still world champion. It was not until he had returned to Oklahoma that he started to complain that I had caused his injury with a deliberate butt

Once I became world champion, Buchanan said some quite complimentary things about me, but deep down he must resent the acclaim I have received. He never got the chance to defend the world title in Scotland and that surely cuts deep with him when he sees the way I have been promoted in front of my own fans. I can understand how he feels but it saddened me to see him making a comeback and chasing lost glories. He should have stayed in retirement and not risked damage to his reputation as one of Scotland's sporting heroes.

According to well-publicized stories, Buchanan ran into business problems. He had my sympathy because his money had been hard-earned in the ring and to lose it in what can be a cruel business world must have hurt him more than any punches he had taken.

I just wish we had been able to fight each other when we were both at the peak of our powers. We would have made a fortune together and I have no hesitation in saying that I would have won. But I'm sure Ken has a different opinion.

And how's this for a punchline: I recently went to buy a kilt and discovered that the Watt Clan wear the Buchanan Tartan!

I was not despondent after my defeat by Buchanan. He was the top contender for the world championship and I had taken him to a narrow points decision. Jim Murray talked of my becoming an international star and I had visions of commercial shows opening up to me, but I was kidding myself. In my next fight, against Anglo-Scot Johnny Cheshire, I found myself back on the club circuit.

Cheshire was an accomplished fighter and had been ABA featherweight champion in 1968, the year that I won the lightweight title. He was No. 3 contender for the British professional championship and when I clearly outpointed him at the Midlands Sporting Club on 9 May 1973, Jim Murray immediately started pressing my claims for a return with Buchanan. But Buchanan had achieved his target of winning a coveted Lonsdale Belt outright and was more interested in trying to regain the world title than a second set-to with me. He wasn't a bad judge.

There was little sign of any more action coming my way, so Murray decided he would promote his own shows in Glasgow to keep me employed. He started giving away free photographs of me in an effort to give me some sort of identity, but I was still virtually unknown outside Scotland because thirteen of my fights had been in private clubs. I desperately needed projection on public shows which were as rare in Glasgow as ice-skating in the Sahara.

On the first of Murray's promotions I again stopped Noel McIvor with a cut eye. That was in June 1973. It was October before I fought again, with Murray inviting my fellow Glaswegian, Angus McMillan, to try his luck against me at Govan Town Hall. Murray at least knew there would be a lot of people at the ringside. Angus had six brothers, all of them boxers, cheering him on.

I had to climb off the canvas to beat Angus after taking the first count of my professional career in the first round. I was more surprised than hurt when a right hook dropped me backwards on to the seat of my trunks. But I was up at three and managed to clear my head during the interval, thanks to the traditional shock water treatment from Murray, who sponged my face with the urgency of a man putting out a fire. McMillan fought a brave, aggressive battle but I found it easy to pick him off with sharp counterpunches as he came forward. At the end of eight fast rounds I was a comfortable points winner. I had just about won Angus outright, having also beaten him four times as an amateur.

I had eliminated all the top British title contenders and was left, once again, kicking my heels while Ken Buchanan kept the championship in cold storage. The only work I could now get was abroad.

Round 12

A Journey of Discovery

Jim Murray and I started to drift apart the day he arranged for me to go to South Africa to fight. Alone.

It was my first experience of boxing abroad as a professional, a big enough ordeal without the extra pressure of having to manage my own affairs. Murray's mother was unwell and I sympathized with him wanting to stay with her in Glasgow. A joiner by trade and a part-time manager, Murray is such a loner in boxing that there was nobody he could send with me in his place and he preferred to let the South African promoters organize training facilities.

As it turned out, it was a journey of discovery for me. I found out that I could handle things for myself perfectly well and even discovered that I was a better negotiator than my manager.

I was paid £1000 for a ten-round fight against South African lightweight champion Andries Steyn, who at the time was ranked eighth in the world ratings. He had once been stopped in three rounds by my old rival Ken Buchanan, but had re-established himself with victories over two former world champions. The South Africans were carefully grooming him for a world championship challenge and I was supposed to be playing just a walk-on part like an Indian on the set of a John Wayne movie. But I wrecked the script by stopping Steyn in seven rounds after opening a nasty gash over his left eye. Steyn claimed I caused the damage with a butt. I prefer to think I did it with a ripping right hook. It was a highly satisfying victory that lifted me to the brink of the world ratings.

The South Africans really took to me and I was invited to

stay on in Johannesburg for a holiday. They pressed me to make my stay permanent by emigrating and said they would be willing to coax Buchanan to come out to South Africa for a return match. It amused me to think we couldn't get promoters interested in putting us together on a commercial show in Scotland and yet here, 7000 miles away in South Africa, they were keen to put us in the same ring. I was given VIP treatment by promoter Jaap de Villiers and local trainer John Middleton helped me keep in trim. Dunky Jowett, in Johannesburg with Scottish bantamweight champion John Kellie, gave me valuable assistance in the corner.

Early on I was asked by a rival promotion group whether I would break my holiday and fight former South African champion Kokkie Olivier. They were desperate to stage the contest and offered me £1000. I said I wouldn't fight Laurence Olivier for that. I knew how anxious they were to get Kokkie to use me as a stepping-stone into the world ratings and I told them I would only consider taking the fight if they paid me a purse of £2000. Their next offer was £1500, but I insisted that it had to be £2000. My business brain told me I had them over a barrel because without me they didn't have a fight and their show was barely two weeks away.

After a lot of deliberation they decided they would telephone Jim Murray in Glasgow. I was lucky enough to get him on the phone first and told him the situation and stressed that under no circumstances should he agree for me to fight for less than £2000. I knew they were ready to meet my demand and all it would have taken from Murray was confirmation that the asking price was right. An hour or so later the promoters informed me that my manager had agreed for me to take the fight with Olivier. For a purse of £1800. I had a furious row with Murray over that. It was not the £200 that bothered me, but the fact that he had been out-negotiated in a deal where he held all the cards.

The March 1974 show was being run by the Toweels, a famous South African fighting family, and they celebrated clinching the fight as if they had already won it. But I clicked into top gear against Olivier and jabbed him silly on the way to a convincing ten-round points victory. One of the Johannesburg newspapermen described my performance as 'one of the finest exhibitions seen in South Africa for many years.'

An odd thing happened to me at the end of the ninth round that was quite scarey. For the one and only time in my life I got an attack of the shakes. My arms and legs started jumping around of their own accord as I sat on my stool preparing myself for the final round. All I could put it down to was the fact that Olivier must have landed a punch on a nerve during the ninth round when he had thrown everything into a do-or-die victory effort. The shaking stopped the moment I left my stool and I have never experienced anything like it again.

I had rarely boxed better in my life than that night in Johannesburg and the promoters were so pleased that they invited me to return the following season. It had been an important trip for me because I had really learned to look after myself. The questioning seed had been sown in my mind. Did I need a manager?

Meantime, back home, there was some title chasing to be done.

In June 1974 I travelled to Caerphilly to meet Welshman Billy Waith in a twelve-round final eliminator for the British title held by Buchanan, who had since added the European crown to his collection. I won an important psychological advantage at the weigh-in by kidding Waith that I was having weight problems. Weight-watching is almost a way of life for me when I am in training for a fight and I become fanatical about making sure I weigh in bang on the 9 st 9 lb limit and certainly never more than eight ounces inside. I have got it down to a fine art and insist on always having scales available so that I can check my weight after and sometimes during meals. Before any title fight, I like to get myself down to 9 st 7 lb on the eve of the contest. Then I can have the satisfaction of sitting down to a good three-course meal, knowing that I will wake up on the morning of the fight weighting around 9 st 10 lb. I have a chart showing the calorie count for a wide range of foods. For instance, I know that if I have minestrone soup, steak with cauliflower, broccoli, two roast potatoes and an ice-cream dessert, I will put on four pounds. The last thing I do before going to bed is weigh myself. If I find I am right on target, I go to the bathroom and have a pee into a glass. I then fill another glass with the exact amount of water as the liquid that has left my body and drink it. Then I sleep well, knowing that in the morning I will weigh 9 st 10 lb. I get rid of that extra pound by having another pee shortly before the official weigh-in.

Against Waith, I decided to pretend I was worried about my weight and deliberately went to the scales half a pound over the 9 st 9 lb limit. You should have seen the look on the faces of promoter Eddie Thomas, Waith's manager Mac Williams and even my own manager, Jim Murray. 'What have you gone and done?' said Murray, with panic in his eyes. This was at the time when we were beginning to drift apart and I hadn't divulged my little plan to him. Thomas, himself a former champion boxer, looked ready to tear his hair out and insisted: 'Take your shorts off. You might just be inside then.'

But I just told everybody to be patient and disappeared to the loo for three minutes. I had deliberately not had a pee that day and by the time I had relieved myself I was down to 9 st 8¾ lb. It was enough of a theatrical act to make Waith think I was weak at the weight while in actual fact I was feeling as strong as an ox. That night I outboxed the Welshman, which was quite a feat because I rate him as clever a craftsman as I have ever met in the ring. Billy is a master of the now-you-see-me-now-you-don't tactics and is as difficult to catch as a Paris pickpocket. He has first-class ring technique and only the lack of a big punch stopped him moving up into world championship contention. I found him a really elusive target but always managed to stay a move and a thought ahead of him and finished a clear points winner.

Ken Buchanan was just as elusive but this was *outside* the ring. He had no intention of giving me a crack at the title and messed me around for months. In exasperation, I agreed to return to South Africa for an October date with non-white South African champion Tony Morodi.

Just before I left for Johannesburg – surprise, surprise – Buchanan announced that he was relinquishing the British championship to concentrate on his bid for the world crown. I could see the sense of his decision, but he should have made it months earlier and saved a lot of aggravation. It had been twenty-two months since we had last contested the title and the British lightweight division had just been brought to a standstill by his selfish attitude.

I was matched with Johnny Cheshire for the vacant crown, but first had to honour my agreement to fight Morodi in Johannesburg. Our fight made history. It was the first time that a black South African boxer had been allowed to meet a white opponent in South Africa. In view of the delicate situation over there, I made no great fuss when the ten-round points decision went against me, even though I'm convinced I won six of the rounds. I don't know who was more amazed when the verdict was announced – Morodi or me. In my heart I know that in three fights in South Africa I scored three victories and I just shrugged the verdict off as 'one of those things'.

The title fight with Cheshire was staged at the St Andrew's Sporting Club on 27 January 1975 – two years all but two days since I had lost the championship to Buchanan at the same venue. I thought referee Wally Thom should have stopped the fight in the sixth round when I dropped Johnny for two long counts and had him in all sorts of trouble. My heart went out to him for the tremendous courage he showed in not giving in and he was trying to battle his way back into the fight when the ref stopped it near the end of the seventh.

Terry Spinks, Cheshire's Cockney trainer and himself a former Olympic and British champion, was furious when the referee led Johnny back to his corner. 'What's the game coming to?' fumed Spinks. 'Is it a sport for pansies now where a fight is stopped just because a boxer is taking a couple of lefts to the face?'

I agree that Johnny was having a go back at me in the seventh and had shaken me with a long left hook, but he was fighting a lost cause and I landed five lefts without reply before the ref stepped in. The wonder was I was able to fight at all. Just a week previously I had been suffering from flu symptoms and had been unable to spar because of a bruised hand. The Lonsdale Belt was clasped around my waist by none other than my old foe Ken Buchanan. The Belt had been loaned to the St Andrew's Sporting Club for the evening by Maurice Hope. Mine was still on order and I was determined to win it outright.

My reward for winning the title was to be nominated to fight Nigerian Jonathan Dele for the vacant Commonwealth championship. British promoters didn't exactly fall over themselves to stage the contest and it was arranged for Lagos on 3 May 1975.

I had a warm-up fight at the Anglo-American Sporting Club in Mayfair's Hilton Hotel and I don't mean this as any disrespect to Billy Waith, but it was a big anticlimax when he was brought in as a late substitute. I had been preparing to meet my first American opponent, New York taxi driver Saoul Mamby, who later proved his class by becoming the world light-welterweight champion. He pulled out at the last minute and Waith and I didn't exactly set the place alight with our long-distance non-title clash that I comfortably won on points.

And so to Lagos where I produced the one performance in my career of which I am ashamed. For the one and only time in my life I failed to even try to give of my best in the ring and I was outpointed by Dele over fifteen untidy and unsatisfactory rounds.

It remains a mystery what happened to me that night. The promoters did their best, but were total novices at running major shows. They fixed me up with training quarters that didn't have a ring and I finished up working out in an army barracks. Because of an airport strike, we had to sleep four to a three-bedded hotel room. The fight was in doubt up to the last minute because of a dispute over rates for the stadium. The promotors thought they could stage the contest under football floodlights and it wasn't until a few hours before the show that they got proper ring lights fixed up. I let all of these irritations get to me and my attitude was all wrong.

Danny Holland joined Jim Murray in my corner and neither of them could do anything to motivate me. I got stuck in a defensive rut and couldn't get out of it. I could make excuses, such as the trouble I was having with my left hand. It had been giving me a lot of pain for several months and I had to have a course of injections. But there was no real excuse or explanation for my miserable performance. I fought with survival rather than victory in mind and at the final bell I knew that Dele had won a narrow but deserved points victory. He was a strong and aggressive fighter, but I know that on a good night I would have given him a boxing lesson.

Some of the reporting of the local journalists left a little to be desired. It was wrongly reported that during the fight I had taken a count of eight. The only time I was off my feet was when both Dele and I got into a tangle and fell to the canvas together. It was *that* sort of fight.

I was amused at the way I was quoted before the fight in one of the Lagos papers: 'I come to Lagos to send Dele to the dentist. I gonna hit him hard on the face and mouth and clear his teeth. I have so much trained hard that I'm sure I'm gonna win even though Dele is as fast as lightning.' I *had* much trained hard, but felt like an empty shell in the ring.

There was now a growing wall of indifference separating me from Jim Murray. The close relationship we had maintained over more than twelve years was damaged beyond repair and we had lost the art of communication that is so vital to a successful manager–boxer relationship. He seemed to fail to understand that I had become an adult and continued to talk to me on the same level as he had when first taking me under his wing as a youngster.

I concede that it was not all one-sided. Murray had his moods and what was almost a persecution complex about the way he felt cold-shouldered in the professional boxing world. But I must also carry some of the blame for our differences because deep down I felt that he just didn't have the knowhow to get me the right fights at the right venues and for the right purses. This made me feel resentful.

It is true that he had guided me to the British title, a fight for the Commonwealth championship and into the reckoning for the European crown. But it had been uphill much of the way. I had been a pro for seven years and had only once boxed on a major London show. It had certainly not been a get-rich-quick existence.

I could see myself falling into the same rut as Ken Buchanan, always having to go abroad for my fights. This didn't suit me at all because Arthur Morrison and I had just started our car repair business and I wanted to be away from Glasgow as rarely as possible. It would have been a different thing if I had been making a fortune from boxing, but a big financial jackpot looked about as likely as an oil strike in Sauchiehall Street.

Margaret and I had just settled down with our growing family at a pleasant house in Moodiesburn and I wanted to ease the weight of my mortgage by earning some quick money in the ring. After my experience in South Africa, I was beginning to think I would be better off managing my own affairs for what I reckoned would be the last two or three fights of my career.

My final break with Murray came after I felt I had been cheated of a points victory in a European championship eliminator against Frenchman André Holyk. The fight was staged in Lyons and even the French fans booed and jeered the split decision in Holyk's favour. Holyk himself was so convinced that I had won that he raised my arms at the final bell.

By then, Murray and I were no longer on friendly terms. We were simply doing business together and all the pleasure and enjoyment had gone out of our relationship. I knew we had gone as far as we could together. The alleged defeat by Holyk had knocked all the ambition, the heart and the confidence out of me and I knew Murray could no longer give me the motivation that I needed.

I don't want anybody putting this book down thinking I have been anything less than fair with my praise and gratitude for all that Murray did for me. He gave me a strong foundation, matched me wisely and filled me with confidence and inspiration at times in my career when I might easily have given up boxing for a less exacting sport. But now there was a broken bridge between us and there was no way for either of us to cross it and go back to the way we were.

Things turned nasty between us after I had refused to box an exhibition on a show he was promoting. I personally feel that exhibitions are something of a 'con' on the public and I didn't want to do it on principle. I went along to the show and he completely ignored me, walking past me as if I didn't exist. That was the point of no return.

There was still a year of my contract to run and Murray said he would only let me go if I agreed to pay £1500 for my release. 'You must be joking!' I said. 'If I can't make money with you I'm blowed if I'll pay to get rid of you.' I threatened to go to the British Boxing Board of Control to plead my case for freedom, but then we agreed on a compromise, Murray stating he would let me go after I had made a scheduled title defence against the then British light-welterweight champion Joey Singleton.

The Singleton fight was called off and Murray started to make plans for another contest, but I insisted that we had reached the end of the road. We shook hands and parted and, sadly, have not exchanged a word since. I hope that one day we can get together and talk over old times like the friends that we should be rather than the passing strangers that we have become.

I have heard it whispered that Murray thought I had been approached by Terry Lawless *before* I made the break with him. This is not true. For several years I had been receiving quiet hints from managers that they would like to handle my career. Terry Lawless was not among them. I had made up my mind to manage myself and even went so far as to fix myself up with a non-title fight against Jimmy Revie. My target was two or three more contests, some quick money in the bank and then retirement to concentrate on my car repair business.

Then I made a telephone call to Terry Lawless that was to lead me to becoming a modern Cinderella Man of the ring. The original Cinderella Man, James J. Braddock, came off the breadline during the Depression in the 1930s and won the world heavyweight championship. I wasn't exactly on the breadline, but Terry turned me into a hungry fighter and then led me to the banqueting table.

Round 13

War of Nerves

I prepare my mind as well as my body for fights and for a month before a contest I become a difficult person to live with because all my thought processes are concentrated on the battle ahead. I suppose it is a form almost of self-hypnosis, mentally preparing myself for a job that allows for no outside interference or intrusion. I become totally self-centred and people apart from those closest to me find it nigh impossible to communicate with me once I am mentally locked into a fight.

The Yoga training I received early in my career from Jim Murray has helped me develop my concentration and Terry Lawless encourages a routine that allows as much time for private thought as physical preparation. This 'locking in' technique starts from the moment I arrive at the Lawless home in Romford, Essex, four weeks before each of my major fights. I drive myself so hard in training that I can sleep for twelve hours in a day, no problem. Terry calls me Rip Van Watt!

One of my biggest psychological weapons is the strength and sound of my Scottish support. The bagpipes and the Scots roar give me a huge advantage when I fight in my homeland. Since becoming champion, I have insisted on my title defences being in Glasgow for tactical as well as patriotic reasons. They say the Hampden roar is worth a goal start to Scotland in football matches. Well I reckon the Scots support is worth a two-round start to me in world championship contests.

I *need* the vocal support of my supporters and consider it a team effort, with me in the ring as their representative and them giving me the motivation to produce my very best on their behalf. The Mexicans are masters at making crowd support an extra weapon. Mickey Duff tells the story that when Alan Rudkin went to California to challenge Ruben Olivares for the world bantamweight title they made a great drama out of putting armed bodyguards round him to protect him from the hostile Mexican supporters. As Rudkin was about to leave the dressing-room, one of the bodyguards said with well-rehearsed timing: 'Don't let the crowd worry you. They'll have to shoot us first before they can get to you.' They were not exactly the most confidence-boosting words for Alan to hear as he was preparing to go to the ring and, not surprisingly, he failed in his title bid. We don't go that far to put fear into the opposition, but the roar of the Scots crowd and the skirl of the pipes certainly has a deflating effect on opponents not accustomed to the fierce patriotism and fanaticism of a Scottish crowd.

My supporters played an important part in helping me win against Texas-based Mexican Roberto Vasquez in my first defence of the world title in Kelvin Hall on 3 November 1979. Vasquez froze when he heard the way the crowd got behind me to a man. As I followed the pipers into the ring I thought to myself, 'Oh no, these people want me to die for them again'. The noise they made was enough to shake Kelvin Hall to its foundations and I think it terrified my boyish-looking twenty-one-year-old opponent.

It was the least satisfying of my world title fights. I could sense from the opening seconds that Vasquez was feeling apprehensive about the size of the job facing him and I immediately went to work to keep him discouraged. The stocky Mexican adopted the strange tactics of continually retreating to the corners of the ring where he was a sitting target for the cluster-punching technique that I had perfected at the Lawless Academy of Boxing.

The challenger came into the ring with a reputation of being a fearsome puncher but I didn't give him the opportunity to land more than half a dozen solid blows throughout nine one-sided rounds. I was bombing punches into the head and body without reply when Californian referee Rudi Ortega quite properly intervened to save Vasquez from being seriously hurt.

I had done all that was asked of me, but was left feeling frustrated because I knew in my heart that Vasquez had not provided world-class opposition. A lot of the ringside reporters dismissed it as a monumental mismatch, but not too many of them had said anything like that *before* the fight when every paper I read warned of his devastating punching power.

Vasquez earned the fight too early for his own good and I hope that I didn't knock the heart out of him. He took a fearful hiding that night. A combination of my aggression and the crowd's passionate support drained him of any will to win.

There was an amusing little cameo on the eve of the fight. José Suleiman, respected President of the World Boxing Council, joined us for dinner at our hotel and was on a strict fish and fruit diet. He just couldn't believe it when he saw me tucking into my usual three-course meal, including steak and potatoes. 'I'm putting on pounds just watching you eat,' he said. José had been accustomed to seeing fighters on weight watcher diets of poached eggs and sugarless tea.

Apart perhaps from that Classics master Lester Piggott, I doubt if there is anybody in top-line sport as weight conscious as I am, but I have got my training routine so well organized that I never have to get in the situation where I need to starve myself. In that respect, I am *not* a hungry fighter.

Once I have got myself mentally right for a fight I then concentrate on my opponent and try to think of weaknesses where I can score vital psychological points. It is the 'dirty tricks' department, but all is fair in love and war. And in boxing.

There are few nicer guys in sport than Charlie Nash, the fighter from Northern Ireland's Bogside. He was my opponent for my second world title defence and I deliberately started a war of nerves with him because I knew that he tended to get worried and nervous before a fight. I decided to play on this weakness.

For more than two years promoters had been trying to get us into the ring together. There were some ill-advised people who made it known that they thought I was frightened of fighting Charlie after I had three times pulled out of scheduled contests with him. Charlie made the mistake of believing it himself and started saying silly things like, 'What kind of a man is Watt to keep avoiding me?'

I made a note of all the things he had been saying about me and then started throwing them back in his face in the build-up to our world championship fight at Kelvin Hall on 14 March 1980. I even invented a few insults of my own that I pretended he had said. 'On the night of the fight I will make Charlie really regret all the insulting things he has been saying about me,' I told every pressman who came to interview me. I knew I had got Charlie rattled when he tried to retract some of the things he had been quoted as saying, but I was determined to keep up the pretence of being fighting mad with him. I made such a thing of my 'hate' campaign against Charlie that I was able to keep secret from all the boxing writers that I was carrying a training injury that almost forced a postponement of the fight.

For seven weeks before the fight I had been in pain from strains in my groin and back. After having failed to keep three fight dates with Charlie, there was no way in the world that I could pull out for a fourth time. I would never have been able to live it down. Without a soul in Glasgow knowing, I went to Ibrox for daily treatment from Rangers phsyiotherapist Tom Craig, and I was given a nine-day course of injections to clear the injury. It severely handicapped my preparation work but I had no doubts that I could conquer Charlie and told Terry not to even consider calling the fight off.

Terry and I watched a video film of his European championship points victory over Ken Buchanan in Denmark and we were both convinced that he did not have sufficient variety of punches to take my title away. I was determined to get Charlie Nash out of my path once and for all.

Perhaps I was *too* determined because I carelessly walked into a sweeping right-hander from Charlie in the first round and was sent tumbling to the canvas. I was annoyed rather than hurt and jumped straight up without a count. It proved the worst thing he could have done to me. I was suddenly wide awake and determined to forget my usual reconnaissance work. I have rarely been so mean in the ring as I was that night with Charlie. He stood between me and what I knew would be a big pay day against Howard Davis. After the fight I learned that Margaret had run out of the hall in terror when Charlie put me on the seat of my trunks. She need not have worried. I was in full control of myself and after that hectic first round also took full control of the fight.

My pre-fight psyching of Charlie had done the trick. He just folded up under my relentless pressure and, handicapped by a gash over his left eye, had no answer when I unleashed my best punches in the fourth round. I knocked him down three times and left referee Sid Nathan with no alternative but to come to his rescue after two minutes ten seconds of the fourth. The thing I remember as I hammered him around the ring in that final round was the sound of my all-time favourite sportswoman Mary Peters screaming at the ringside. 'Charlie!' she shouted. 'Oh, Charlie . . .!'

When the fighting was all over and Charlie had recovered his senses, I confessed to him that I had not really meant any of the nasty things I had been saying to him and about him. If he had won the world championship it would not have happened to a nicer bloke. But I was in no mood to let him have it.

Now I was ready for the man whose name was beginning to haunt me: Howard Davis.

Round 14

Flower of Scotland

There were a lot of people in boxing who considered me just a pretender to the throne. Almost from the moment I became champion, the name of Howard Davis was being rammed at me like a poisoned dagger. Davis had been the Golden Boy of the 1976 Montreal Olympics, beating the likes of Sugar Ray Leonard, Teofilo Stevenson and the Spinks brothers to the Best Stylist award. It was with a sense of relief rather than concern when I was finally matched with him. It rankled me that outside Britain I was still something of an unknown warrior, even though I had been world champion for more than a year. I knew that I could make a name for myself off the back of Davis. Once I had beaten him, nobody would ever again refer to me as Jim Who.

Maestro Mickey Duff cleverly outmanoeuvred the American promoters to clinch the Davis fight for Scotland. They were desperate to put it on in the States where Davis had a massive following because of his build-up on CBS television which had screened every one of his professional fights. After hours of trans-Atlantic phone calls and trips to and from New York, Mickey finally managed to get a package deal together that was boosted by a huge offer from the ABC television company. They are the cut-throat rivals of CBS and knew it would be prime upmanship if they could show Davis challenging for the world championship after his massive projection on the other channel. It was like BBC trying to poach Len Fairclough from ITV!

Mickey flew to Mexico City with Boxing Board secretary Ray Clarke for the opening of the purse offers at the World Boxing Council headquarters. Dennis Rappaport and Mike

Jones, New York landlords and joint managers of Davis, were also there and fully confident that an American bid would clinch the fight. But they had underestimated Mickey's negotiating skill. 'You could almost hear the thud as their faces hit the floor when it was announced that our bid had come out top,' Mickey recalls when telling the story of how he won me the fight of a lifetime.

Barrett–Duff Promotions had already pulled off a coup before Mickey went to Mexico. He and Mike Barrett knew that Kelvin Hall would not house enough spectators to finance the fight and so they approached Rangers Football Club and, thanks largely to the cooperation of manager John Greig, got the go-ahead to stage the world championship show at Ibrox Park. They even lined up world junior lightweight champion Alexis Arguello as a top-flight substitute in case Davis refused to come to Scotland to challenge me. Reluctantly, the American's managers agreed to the fight being put on in Glasgow and the match was made for the evening of 7 June 1980. It was to be the first outdoor fight in Scotland for twenty years.

A few weeks before the contest I was given every incentive to win when I was quietly asked if I would be willing to accept the award of an MBE in the Queen's Birthday Honours list which was to be announced the week after the fight. It was a wonderful tribute to me and to my sport and I naturally agreed to have my name put forward for the honour. What I knew in my heart was that if I lost I would ask to have my name removed from the list. I decided I only deserved the award if I was still champion of the world.

Following the tragic death of my darling sister-in-law, Joyce, I had to dig deeper than ever into my mental resources to find the necessary concentration for the fight. I gathered my grief and pushed it away into a far corner of my mind. It took enormous self-discipline, but as a professional fighter I had a vital job of work ahead of me and just one slip of concentration could prove fatal. My tears came later and privately.

Once I had joined Terry in London, the fight became my one and only concern. In training I was lucky to have a stablemate as talented and skilful as Kirkland Laing, who did a superb impersonation of Davis in round after round of sparring.

Terry and I spent hours studying video films of Davis in action. There could be no argument that he was a naturally gifted boxer with fast fists and clever but flashy ring movement. On talent alone, he was a better equipped boxer than I was. But I knew an area where I had him licked. Experience.

His big weakness was that he had fought only thirteen times as a professional and this was the territory where I aimed to score psychological points. I allowed him to do all the pre-fight talking and the wider he opened his mouth the better I liked it. He may have been able to do the business with his fists, but he was a novice when it came to using his mouth. Davis was a very poor imitation of Muhammad Ali and made me genuinely angry with some of his statements.

A lot of insults are thrown in boxing to help sell tickets. I have often manufactured malice to boost the box office business and also, as in the case of Charlie Nash, to put psychological pressure on my opponent. With Davis it was different. He had been bad-mouthing me from a platform of contempt.

'Jim Who?' he kept saying, making it clear that in his opinion I was just a nobody minding what he considered was rightfully *his* world title. But a championship has to be won in the ring and I was going to make him regret his scornful references to me. One of his quotes that really upset me was, 'You can cut off both my legs, both my arms, blindfold me, put a cigarette in my mouth and I'll *still* beat him.'

This arrogant young man had gone too far and I gave a lot of thought as to how I could play on his nerves. I decided to hold back my best verbal shots until just before the fight. At a press conference three days before we were due to climb into the ring, I sowed the first seeds of doubt in his mind that perhaps the championship contest was not going to be the easy job he had led himself to expect.

He wanted to be friendly at the conference but I didn't want to know. 'He's been talking too much,' I said. 'I'll make him pay for all the stupid things he's been saying. I'll do my talking in the ring with my fists where and when it matters.'

Davis, along with quite a few of my press pals, was surprised by my aggressive attitude. He tried to laugh it off but then I hit him in the mind where it hurts.

'You have never had a fifteen-round fight in your life,' I said. 'This will be my fourteenth fifteen-rounder. You've not even had that many fights.'

I had been saving this point up. No matter who you are and how good you are, the first time you go into a fifteen-round fight you wonder to yourself, 'Will I be able to last the distance?' When you first step up from three-round amateur contests, you worry about being able to last the six-rounds course. You have the same worry when you move up to eight and then to ten rounds. Davis had never been more than ten rounds. The thought of going fifteen in only his fourteenth professional fight must have been terrifying him.

I'm sure he didn't sleep too well that night of our press conference. He had been surrounded by overconfident people who looked on me as a cardboard champion. I was the first person he had heard make the point that just maybe I was not going to be the pushover he had been primed to expect.

The promotion proved one long headache for Mickey Duff and Mike Barrett. Rappaport and Jones, relative newcomers to boxing who had managed Davis since his Olympic triumph, were, to put it mildly, a pain in the buttocks. They didn't give the expected cooperation in publicizing the fight and even cast doubts as to whether it would take place. On the eve of the Saturday show they kicked up a storm over the weight of the gloves being used. They walked out of a rules meeting and rumours flashed right around Glasgow that the fight was off. Finally they conceded that, as originally agreed, we would wear six-ounce rather than eight-ounce gloves. But they made such a fuss that I wonder how many thousands were knocked off the attendance because of the threat that the fight would be called off?

There was talk after the fight of writs over the uncooperative attitude of the Americans. Rappaport and Jones threatened Mickey Duff with an eight-million-dollar law suit because I had agreed to take much less than the reported purse of £500,000. Mickey countersued and as I prepare this book the bitter legal fighting is still going on.

The fighting *inside* the ring was much cleaner and more sporting. Heavy rain and those pre-fight rows kept the attendance down to 12,000, but the crowd made so much noise on my behalf that Ibrox sounded as if there were a Rangers goal being scored every minute. Davis and I had an eyeball-to-eyeball confrontation before the first bell. It was out of character for me, but it has become an expected and accepted part of the American fight scene and I was determined to show Davis that I was in no mood to back down.

I fought to a controlled and carefully thought-out fight pattern. Everybody assumed I would make the cautious start that has become almost a trademark, but I went powering in from the first bell and surprised Davis with my speed and positive punching. He was much stronger and braver than I expected and I soon realized that I was not going to be able to break his heart and his will. By the halfway mark I had built up a good lead with a procession of jabs that I kept in a queue on the end of his nose. He was throwing more leather than me, but many of his punches were out of range and I was able to catch a lot of them on my arms and gloves. The tenth and eleventh rounds were the only ones during the fight when I felt anything less than in command. He caught me with his head in the tenth and opened a cut under my left eye. This gave him his first real encouragement and he put me under heavy pressure in the eleventh and won the round.

Davis did a silly thing as the bell rang at the end of the eleventh. He raised his arms high in a gesture of triumph. His arrogance gave me an extra spark and I came out in the twelfth determined to reassert my authority on the fight. The crowd lifted their support to new peaks and their cheering, chanting and singing acted like a whiff of oxygen.

Terry was keeping a careful round-by-round score and told me just before the start of the fourteenth that a good round would virtually put the fight out of Davis's reach. It gave me the motivation to drag extra effort from my tired body and I had my best round of the fight. I trapped Davis in a neutral corner and hammered away at him non-stop for a full minute. That was the fight virtually over for both of us. I was exhausted from hitting him and he was exhausted from being hit and trying to get out of the way of my punches. Neither of us had sufficient strength and energy left in the fifteenth round to do anything startling and at the final bell we fell into each other's arms and embraced like long-lost brothers. As we stood with our arms wrapped round each other, we experienced a bond of sportsmanship and a depth of feeling that only two boxers who have just done battle will fully understand. We had won each other's respect.

More important to me, I had won a battle to establish my identity. Never again would I mockingly be referred to as Jim Who. There were 400 million television viewers around the world who now knew that Jim Watt's my name.

I had the immense satisfaction of being awarded a unanimous points decision and the only mystery to everybody was how that excellent Filippino referee, Carlos Padilla, made me a winner by only one point. My victory was a lovely smack in the eye for the Scottish bookmakers who ran out of faith in me and made Davis the pre-fight favourite.

On impulse, I took the microphone and led my marvellous supporters in an emotional rendering of 'Flower of Scotland'. I sang from the heart because at that moment there was not a prouder Scot in the whole wide world.

This flower of Scotland had finally blossomed.

Round 15

My Finest Hour

My world title defence against Sean O'Grady at Kelvin Hall on 1 November 1980, was surrounded by so much drama and controversy that it would take a report from a war correspondent to do it full justice.

There has never been a fight quite like it in Britain. For a start, it was arranged for two o'clock in the morning to tie in with American television which wanted to screen the contest live to an evening audience. There was quite a bit of criticism from newspapermen over this, with *Sunday People* columnist Mike Langley making the point that he didn't hold with boxers defending world titles when they ought to be in bed. But I am sure Mike and his colleagues would willingly produce a newspaper in the middle of the night if they were told their wages would be trebled! I didn't particularly relish the thought of fighting at two o'clock in the morning but American television paid heavily for keeping me awake. I am a professional and am more concerned about the money in the purse than the hands on the clock. I got laughs with the cheap joke: 'Let's face it, two o'clock in the morning is the usual time for fights to start in Glasgow. . . .'

Mickey Duff claims he has never had a tougher time getting a fight together. He had to negotiate not only with Pat O'Grady, Sean's father, manager and a former fighter, but also his mother Jean, who was nicknamed the Annie Oakley of boxing. By the time the O'Gradys had held Mickey to ransom, he felt as if he had been assaulted by the James gang. He finally clinched the fight with barely three weeks left to publicize it and sell the tickets. But Mickey's headaches were only just beginning.

I made my usual trek down to London to prepare for the fight with Terry Lawless. We turned our timetable upside down so that we could get adjusted both mentally and physically to fighting at New York time. Terry wore two watches on his wrist, one showing British time and the other switched back six hours to correspond with New York clocks. I got into the habit of going to bed at three o'clock in the morning and sleeping through until midday. To pass the time, Terry made video recordings of all our favourite television programmes and we would sit up together watching TV until the wee small hours. It was the first time 'Watch With Mother' has ever been screened at two o'clock in the morning (it was Terry's favourite!).

Our most important viewing sessions came when Terry put on video films of O'Grady in action. He was just twenty-one, but was already a vastly experienced fighter, with a record that on paper made him look almost invincible. In seventy-four fights he had been beaten just once and he had stopped no fewer than sixty-five of his opponents. He clearly carried a bomb of a punch in either hand. You don't knock out nine of your first ten opponents in the first round unless you can bang a bit. But Terry and I drew comfort from the fact that at least sixty of his opponents were no more than so-so fighters. Most of his contests had been promoted by his father in his hometown of Oklahoma and it looked to us as if he had been fed a diet of soft touches. Studying the films of him in action, we could see that he had been involved in so many easy fights that he had picked up bad habits and we noted weaknesses in his defence where I could punish him.

It was also clear that, like me, he was prone to cuts. In the trade, we are known as 'bleeders'. O'Grady had bled so much from eye injuries that he had undergone plastic surgery. He claimed it was only to improve his looks for television, but Terry and I were not to be taken in by that old rhubarb.

As usual I prepared myself for the fight by loading pressure on my shoulders. I committed myself to preparing this book, knowing I would not want to let the publishers down by losing. Then I told every reporter who came to see me that I was determined to beat Benny Lynch's record of most successful world title defences by a Scot. I needed just one more victory to beat the record.

The O'Grady Bunch – a great posse of people including Ma, Pa, brothers, sisters and even Granny O'Grady – had arrived in Glasgow to train for the fight. They made what Terry and I considered the mistake of working out in the gymnasium at 1 a.m. every morning. It meant the fighter was sitting around in his hotel all day with nothing but the fight on his mind. We kept getting stories relayed to us that Pa and Ma were thinking of packing their bags and taking their tribe home. The biggest bust-up came when they objected to the appointment of the three fight officials: referee Raymond Baldeyrou and judges Harry Gibbs of London and Arthur Mercante of New York. All three are among the top half dozen referees in the world and respected throughout the sport for their honesty, integrity and intelligent handling of contests. But Pa O'Grady had complaints about all three of them and talked about heading home. 'It's reverse psychology,' Terry said. 'It's an old trick in boxing. By complaining about the officials you put pressure on them to bend over backwards to treat your fighter fairly. But these are three of the most experienced men in boxing and won't be put off by anything the O'Gradys say or threaten.'

I could sense that the pressure was telling on the O'Grady camp when Pa moaned that they had only three weeks to prepare for the fight. It struck me that they were getting excuses ready for a defeat of their No. 1 son. I laughed when I was told about this grumble and told the press: 'How could they have forgotten that Sean had a fight as short a time ago as 25 September? Does he go out of condition that quickly?'

O'Grady was nicknamed the 'Bubblegum Bomber' because of his liking of bubblegum and his reputation for bombing out opponents. He got a lot of newspaper space with pictures showing him blowing massive gum bubbles and I got a laugh out of Terry when I vowed that O'Grady would come to a sticky end. My business partner Arthur Morrison hit on the bright idea of having badges made for me and my supporters that carried the title, 'The Bubble Burster'.

There had been so much uncertainty about the fight taking

place from the early stages of Mickey Duff's negotiations with the O'Gradys that it would have been easy for me to have switched off and become complacent. But I convinced myself the fight was going ahead from the first moment that the match was made. My theory was simply that it would be better to train and not to fight than to fight and not to have trained.

I was resting in my hotel room with two hours to go to the weigh-in when Terry came in carrying an unusually long face. 'It looks like the fight's off,' he said.

'You must be joking,' I said, but realizing that he was deadly serious.

'Some nut has apparently sent O'Grady a death threat,' Terry explained. 'His old man said they're packing their bags and getting the next flight out of Glasgow. This time he means it.'

Terry had known about the death threat and the possible walk-out for several hours, but had kept it from me rather than destroy my concentration. But the O'Gradys seemed so intent on going home that he felt he had to break the news to me.

'Mickey is with the O'Gradys now,' he said. 'They've got the top police brass there and are trying to convince them that they will have complete protection.'

Just as Terry was telling me that the death threat had allegedly come in a letter from somebody claiming to belong to 'The Protestant Army', Arthur Morrison came to our room.

'The fight's back on,' he said. 'The O'Gradys have agreed to go through with it provided they get police protection and that they can have a private weigh-in at their hotel.'

It later transpired that the death threat had supposedly been made because O'Grady posed for a photograph while wearing a Celtic shirt during a visit to a Celtic match. They are the club with the predominantly Catholic following but they would not have wanted to get involved in nonsense of this kind. There were some distinctly American-sounding phrases in the letter such as 'We're going to get you, man.' Nobody could find the envelope that the letter was said to have arrived in and it was significant that the police quickly dropped their inquiries. Perhaps I have a suspicious mind but I couldn't help thinking that somebody somewhere was trying to unsettle *me* rather than the kid from Oklahoma.

My suspicions were strengthened by O'Grady's composure in the ring before the fight started. He was completely unmoved and unconcerned by the passionate and frenzied welcome I got from my marvellous fans. They gave me the sort of greeting that would have disturbed a man of less nerve and coolness. O'Grady certainly didn't give the appearance of a person who just a few hours earlier had been allegedly terrified by a death threat. He stood in his corner casually blowing bubbles with his gum until just a few seconds before the first bell. It was a performance that gave a whole new meaning to the use of the word gumshield!

O'Grady was two inches taller than me at 5 ft $10\frac{1}{2}$ in and was what we call in the game a good 'on top' fighter. That is that when he is allowed to move forward and dictate the pace and pattern of a fight he can be very effective. My strategy was to keep forcing him back and I set out in the early rounds to take quick command. I never had my right jab out of his face and punished him with heavy two-handed attacks in the second and third rounds. My supporters thought I was in for a comfortable victory and started chanting 'Ea-sy . . . Ea-sy . . .' But they were premature with their victory celebrations.

O'Grady was boxing with commendable restraint and was obviously conserving energy. Most people had expected him to come out throwing big punches, but he was biding his time and searching for openings. Three or four times in those early rounds our heads collided as he tried to stop me forcing him back onto his back foot. Midway through the fourth his head caught me a sickening thump on the bridge of the nose and as I took a pace back he caught me with a solid right uppercut. From that moment on I was bleeding from the nose and every time I took a deep breath I sucked in my own blood. I was having to fight for spells with my mouth open which is a dangerous thing to do because a punch to the jaw could cause a fracture. But I made sure that O'Grady was out of distance before taking great gasps of air.

The American was also cut on the nose, but it was an exterior injury while mine was bleeding from the inside and so making it difficult for Terry to staunch the blood during the minute intervals. I was still controlling the fight, but had more problems in the sixth round when I came out of a clinch with a weeping graze under my right eye.

As in all my fights, I was keeping a mental scorecard in my head and going into the ninth round I reckoned I was at least three or even four rounds in front. I could sense the steam gradually going out of O'Grady who was dangerous with sudden two-fisted flurries, but there was not the snap to his punches that there had been in the sixth and seventh rounds. Two more rounds of right jab treatment, I thought, and then I will release all my ammunition. I reckoned he would be ready to go in about the twelfth round. Then, suddenly and dramatically, my plans were turned upside down.

O'Grady caught me with a ripping left hook as I moved forward to punish him with follow-through lefts after I had opened his defence with a series of about six or seven thumping right jabs. There were suddenly screams from the ringside as spectators saw a spurt of blood. I could feel a warm trickle alongside my right eye and realized it must have been serious from the reaction of the fans and of O'Grady, who visibly grew in confidence. French referee Raymond Baldeyrou stepped in between us with a flutter of his hands and for a split second I thought he was going to stop the fight, but was relieved to see that he was summoning the doctor. A stay of execution. As I stood in my corner, Superpro Terry with an expressionless look on his face wiped the blood away ready for the doctor's inspection and took the opportunity to gently pinch the cut together.

I have never felt sadder in the ring. With my history of cuts, I was convinced my title had gone and as I turned to face Board of Control medical officer, Dr James Shea, I wondered what sort of contingency plans Mickey Duff had made for a return fight with O'Grady. Dr Shea – God bless him – decided the cut was not serious enough to warrant a stoppage and the referee waved us back into action. For the rest of the round I unashamedly ran away from O'Grady. Not out of fear of his punches but because I didn't want him to land either a fist or his head on the injury. I was desperate to hear the bell so that I could get back to my corner for Terry to do his expert repair work on the wound.

What I learned later about those traumatic moments is that Terry had been just a second away from stopping the fight, but then allowed his professionalism to take charge while he waited for the doctor's verdict. Once again, it was too much for Margaret, who was sitting at the ringside with Andrew. She bolted out of the arena closely followed by her best friend, Harriet Griffin, who watched the rest of the fight from the back gangway and kept going out into the corridor to tell Margaret what was happening.

Terry and I had one of the quickest and most vital tactical discussions of our partnership during the minute interval between the ninth and tenth rounds.

'It's a bad cut, Jim,' he confirmed. 'You're not going to have much time in which to win the fight. You either go all out to take him in this round or . . .'

I knew what Terry was going to say and beat him to it. '. . . or I claim the centre of the ring and keep him on the end of my jab,' I said. 'I don't think he's ready to be bombed out yet. I'll try to keep it at long range and see how I go.'

Meantime, Terry had been working on the cut with his swab stick. Frank Black took over as repairman on my nose and on the worsening graze under my right eye, while George Wiggs sponged the back of my neck and massaged my legs. The professionals were at work. There is not a corner team to touch them.

It was in the tenth round that I won the fight and O'Grady lost it. He should have come out and thrown everything at me, but I dictated exactly how the exchanges should go and kept forcing him onto his back foot by continually pumping my right jab into his face. I took up squatter's rights in the centre of the ring so that he could not catch me on the ropes. My guard was high, my gloves protecting my eye and I don't think O'Grady landed more than two or three head punches throughout a round in which he should have called on his youth and strength to try to overpower me. He was either badly advised by his corner or too tired to take advantage of the situation.

Then the sensational turning point. In the last minute of the round O'Grady shaped to throw a left as I let fly with a left cross of my own. I failed to connect and, as we both moved our heads forward with the momentum of our punches, we collided. His head was coming up and mine was going down. It was a complete accident. The last thing I wanted was his head anywhere near mine. But it was O'Grady who came off worse and blood started gushing from a gash high on his forehead.

It was in this instant that O'Grady virtually surrendered the fight. I don't care if my eye had been hanging out, I would have been in there battling to keep my title. But the American stood back and complained to the referee about the head collision. It was a novice-like thing to do and he broke boxing's golden rule: defend yourself at all times. I sent him jolting back into his own corner with a right to the side of the head and a scything left to the body that almost knocked all the wind out of him. I knew there and then that he just didn't want my title badly enough.

We were now equal on cuts, but I was in total control of the fight. I stabbed so many rights into his face that he was blinking from a mixture of their effect and of the blood that was running down from his forehead. It was ugly, barbaric stuff, but a world championship was at stake and this was not a sight for the squeamish.

The doctor was twice called to inspect O'Grady's injury. Dr Shea certainly had his hands full. He had to keep breaking off from treating an unfortunate ringside reporter who had suffered an epileptic fit. O'Grady had lost the will to fight and I sensed he was just waiting for somebody to pull him out of the contest. Dr Shea wouldn't put him out of his misery and, after a second look at the wound in round twelve, judged that the fight could continue.

It had now become sickeningly one-sided and the Glasgow spectators had seen enough of what had developed into one of the bloodiest fights in British boxing history. Coins started coming into the ring and somebody tossed a programme over the ropes in protest. I only saw it out of the corner of my eye and thought O'Grady's corner had thrown in the towel – an act of surrender that is not recognized in Britain. I pummelled a procession of punches into O'Grady's face and was just about to step up my punch rate when the referee, to everybody's relief, decided that the challenger had taken enough punishment.

I felt as if I had lost and regained my world championship all within the space of a few frantic minutes. I have never known a fight or a night quite like it.

In the dressing-room twenty minutes later, after another of our Scottish celebrations during which I somehow managed a chorus of 'Flower of Scotland', Terry said to me in fair impersonation of Churchill: 'This was your finest hour, Jim. I don't know anybody else who could have stayed as composed as you after the nightmare of that ninth round.'

'Terry,' I said, feeling very emotional, 'this was *our* finest hour. I could never have done it without all the work that you, Frank and George did for me in the corner.'

An hour or so later in the casualty department of Glasgow Western Infirmary Sean O'Grady and I sat in adjoining cubicles while doctors stitched our wounds.

'You're quiet in here tonight, Doc,' I commented.

'Aye,' he said. 'All the head cases have been busy watching you fight!'

As he prepared to stitch the deep gash alongside my right eye, I told him: 'Put in as many stitches as you like, Doc. Remember that I want to fight again.'

He put in eight stitches and said he was confident it would heal nice and cleanly.

Terry and I shook hands with Sean O'Grady and his father, Pat. They could not have been friendlier.

'Sorry it had to end that way,' I told Sean. 'You put up a performance of which you can be proud.'

'Thanks, Jim,' he said. 'You're a great champ and I couldn't have lost to a greater fighter. You really surprised me with your strength. I know you didn't mean to catch me with your head. It was a complete accident.'

'Sure it was,' said Pat O'Grady. 'These things happen in boxing. It wasn't deliberate and I want to thank you for having given us the opportunity to fight for the title and I'd like you to thank all your Scottish fans for their fine hospitality.'

He then turned to Terry and said: 'We'd very much like a return. We have no complaints about what happened tonight, but I think Sean did enough to merit another crack at the title.'

'Certainly,' said Terry. 'If satisfactory terms can be arranged we would be willing to give Sean a return here in Glasgow. He did himself proud tonight.'

On our way back to the Albany Hotel, I said to Terry: 'They've taken it surprisingly well.'

Terry nodded his wise head. 'Sure they did to our faces here in Glasgow,' he said. 'But let's wait and see what they say when they are back on their own territory . . .'

Twenty minutes later in the Albany Hotel my dear old Mum sat mopping at my wounds with a damp cloth. 'I hope I never have to do this again, Jim,' she said.

'I know how you feel about things, Mum,' I told her as gently as possible. 'But I'll tell you what I've already told Margaret. Only one person will decide when I should retire. That's got to be me. But I promise I won't put you through much more anguish.'

The retirement theme became a chief talking point in Glasgow for the next week or more. Nobody was trying to talk me into retirement out of spite, but because they were concerned for me and wanted me to get out while I was still on top and still champion of the world.

Everybody was mentioning my age and were suddenly managing to make me, at thirty-two, sound as old as Methuselah. Yet the truth is that I felt younger than five years before when I left Jim Murray while in a mood of depression and thinking that my career was virtually over.

Age is an attitude of mind. People put too much emphasis on figures instead of on feelings. My performance against O'Grady was good enough to warrant me thinking of one or perhaps two more title defences. He was the feared power-puncher of boxing who had been knocking everybody over. Yet his best punches had not shifted me and if it had not been for my eye injury I know I would have beaten him with ease.

Physically and mentally I feel in great shape. I will know when the time is right to step down off the mountain and start catching up on a lot of living that has been sacrificed in the interests of total fitness of both the mind and the body. I am not yet ready for the final bell.

A few days later in Oklahoma, Pat O'Grady made an official protest to the World Boxing Council. He claimed I had deliberately butted his son and that I should be ordered to give him a return fight.

It's what you know in your heart that matters and I have no doubt that I won the fight fair and square. As Terry Lawless said, it was my finest hour.

Thank you for coming the distance with me and I now invite you to dip into my scrapbook . . .

The Jim Watt
Scrapbook 1964–80

This section of my book could have been called 'What the Papers Say'. I have kept cuttings all the way through my career, since my early days as an amateur right up to the present. Many sportsmen say publicly that they don't bother to read what people write about them, but I know that there are few who can privately resist scouring the sports pages, particularly when they know they have produced a good performance. I have several warm friends among the sportswriting fraternity and have generally been treated kindly by the press throughout my long haul to the top. My thanks to the British pressmen who have reported my boxing fortunes, the ups and downs. In particular, I would like to mention Dick Currie of the *Daily Record* and ITV commentator Reg Gutteridge, both of whom helped bring Terry Lawless and me together by encouraging us to have that first vital telephone conversation back in the winter of 1976. In the reports and comments that I quote in the following pages I have endeavoured always to credit the writer and the newspaper but there are one or two instances where the information was not available. Where fights are reported I give the date that the contest took place rather than when the article was published. I am grateful to everybody who has considered me worthy of their words. I needia the media!

Scotland went down 4–3 in an injury-shortened match here in Aalborg tonight after the Danes had astonishingly banned lightweight Jim Watt from boxing against them . . . because he is too good! Watt, eighteen-year-old Glasgow apprentice electrician and Western District champion, was ready to fight

Jutland's Per Falk Christensen in what would have been the eighth bout of the match. But the Danes, who had seen Watt smash his way to a two-minute win in what was his international début in Copenhagen two nights ago, banned him. Their team manager said: 'Our boxer is not good enough to meet Watt. He could be badly hurt and we will not permit the match.'

James Sanderson
Scottish Daily Express
14 January 1968

Jim Watt, Glasgow's nineteen-year-old lightweight, scored a spectacular first-round win in the ABA semifinals at Belle Vue, Manchester, last night. It was a one-punch victory over England's great hope, seventeen-year-old John Stracey, who had previously eliminated the British champion Terry Waller. Watt produced a superb punch – a right cross flush to the jaw – from which Stracey had no hope of rising. His work lasted just forty-five seconds including the count but it was long enough to convince a packed hall that here was a fine successor to Olympic gold medallist Dick McTaggart who boxed at the same weight.

Andrew Clunie
Daily Mail
26 April 1968

I was impressed by the technique and accurate punch placing of Glasgow southpaw Jim Watt who took the ABA lightweight title by clearly outpointing Bristolian Bobby Fisher. He has the style and the composure to take the eyes of the judges in the Mexico Olympics. There were none of the first round fireworks that he produced in the semifinals when dispatching glittering Cockney prospect John Stracey with as good a right-hand punch as has been seen in amateur boxing for many a year. But his all-round ringcraft kept him a thought and a deed ahead of Fisher throughout the three rounds. Watt is one to watch and dare I say that the last Scot to win an

Olympic gold medal back in 1956 was Dick McTaggart, a lightweight and a southpaw.

Reg Gutteridge
London Evening News
10 May 1968

Of all the champions in the history of the ABA championships few can have been more carefully guided to fistic eminence than Jim Watt, Scotland's current lightweight title-holder. With mentor Jim Murray planning the moves, fair-haired, good-looking Watt has come through thirty-seven bouts (four defeats) unmarked. Watt, twenty this month and an apprentice electrician, could have made his debut for Scotland a lot earlier, but invitations to take part in internationals – against South Africa and Russia among others – were declined because Watt was considered too inexperienced. This action more than any other exemplifies Jim Murray's attitude ... the boxer's welfare before all else.

Boxing News
June 1968

Jim Watt, Scotland's hope for an Olympic boxing medal, will *not* take part in the Olympics in Mexico City in October. This sensational news came in a letter from Watt, the ABA lightweight champion, to Mr John Henderson, the general secretary of the Scottish ABA today. From his home in Dunoon, Mr Henderson said: 'This is a sensational development. Watt tells me in his letter that he will never again box at the lightweight poundage of 9 st 7 lb.' Blond-haired southpaw Watt, who caused another sensation with his forty-five seconds KO over the much-fancied Londoner Johnny Stracey in the ABA semi-final, revealed to Mr Henderson that he had been fighting weight trouble all season. Later Watt's coach Jim Murray who has nursed him carefully from his days as a youth champion to becoming one of the best amateurs in Britain, confirmed that Jim will never again box as an amateur lightweight. But when I asked whether this meant a step up to

132

light-welterweight or a move into the professional ring, Murray was non-committal.

John Quinn
Evening Times
20 June 1968

Jim Watt, ABA lightweight champion, has thrown his last punch as an amateur. He has applied for a professional licence and will be managed by Jim Murray, his Cardowan Boxing Club trainer. This was Watt's career record in the amateur division:

1964

28 Jan.	T. Durrie (Rolls-Royce) Paisley	W rsc 1
28 Mar.	D. Wilson (Larkfield) Glasgow (W. District Youth Champs.)	W rsc 1
28 Mar.	T. McGlinchey Glasgow (W. District Youth Champs.)	W rsc 1
4 Apl	G. McIntyre (Hayton) Kirkcaldy (Scottish Youth Champs.)	W rsc 1
4 Apl	A. Harrison (Couper) Kirkcaldy (Scottish Youth Final)	L rsc 2
26 Oct.	J. Steal (Larkhall) Greenock	W pts

1965

10 Apl	W. Kerr (Fir) Glasgow (W. District Youth Champs.)	W pts
10 Apl	P. Harrison (Transport) Glasgow (W. District Youth Champs.)	W pts
17 Apl	G. McIntyre (Hayton) Perth (Scottish Youth Champs.)	W ko 3

17 Apl	F. Croll (St Francis)	W rsc 1
	Perth	
	(Scottish Youth Champs. Final)	
8 May	V. Halpin	W rsc 1
	Glasgow	
	(British Youth Champs.)	
8 May	W. Rogers	W rsc 3
	Glasgow	
	(British Youth Champs.)	
9 Oct.	W. Endall	L pts
	Bulkington	
	(British Youth Champs. Final)	

1966

2 Feb.	J. McNair (Transport)	W pts
	Edinburgh	
	(Scottish Senior Champs.)	
2 Feb.	F. Humphries (Kelvin)	L pts
	Edinburgh	
	(Scottish Senior Champs.)	
12 Mar	A. McMillan (Corinthians)	W pts
	Dalry	
24 Mar.	A. McMillan (Corinthians)	W pts
	Glasgow	
20 Apl.	T. Marshall (Garnock)	W rsc 2
	Hamilton	
17 Nov.	D. Simpson (Whitletts)	W ko 3
	Glasgow	
	(W. District Champs.)	
17 Nov.	A. McMillan (Corinthians)	W pts
	Glasgow	
	(W. District Champs.)	
17 Nov.	D. Bishop (Lanarkshire)	W ko 2
	Glasgow	
	(W. District Final)	
1 Dec.	A. McMillan (Corinthians)	W pts
	Glasgow	

1967

| 3 Mar. | H. McLean (Madison) | W pts |
| | Grangemouth | |

27 Mar.	B. Mitchell (Craigneuk)	W pts
	Dalry	
28 Apl	B. Mitchell (Craigneuk)	W rsc 3
	Motherwell	
9 Oct.	L. Spriggs (Battersea)	L pts
	London	
16 Nov.	D. Bishop (Lanarkshire)	W rsc 2
	Glasgow	
	(W. District Champs.)	
16 Nov.	T. Boyce (Rolls-Royce)	W rsc 1
	Glasgow	
	(W. District Champs.)	
16 Nov.	B. Mallon (Denniston YC)	W pts
	Glasgow	
	(W. District Champs. Final)	

1968

12 Jan.	Jan Nielson	W rsc 1
	Copenhagen	
	(Denmark v. Scotland)	
10 Feb.	W. Black (Leith)	W pts
	Edinburgh	
	(Scottish Champs.)	
10 Feb.	G. McKenzie (Sparta)	W pts
	Edinburgh	
	(Scottish Champs.)	
10 Feb.	P. Harrison (Transport)	W pts
	Edinburgh	
	(Scottish Champs. Final)	
9 Mar.	E. Hendricks	W rtd 2
	Edinburgh	
	(Scotland v. Ireland)	
21 Mar.	H. Hayes (Doncaster)	W pts
	Glasgow	
	(ABA Quarterfinal)	
25 Apl	J. Stracey (Repton)	W ko 1
	Manchester	
	(ABA Semifinal)	
10 May	R. Fisher (Hartcliffe)	W pts
	Wembley	
	(ABA Final)	

Boxing News
July 1968

Glasgow southpaw Jim Watt (9–11½), the former ABA light-weight champion, made a promising debut to his professional career by scoring a fourth round knockout victory over Santos Martins, Ghana (10–0). The twenty-year-old Scot, who turned down the chance of fighting in the recent Olympics, showed up well against his experienced rival. He carried the fight to Martins for the greater part of the action and was always the faster of the two. Martins had a tendency to swing his punches rather than send them home by the direct route and this allowed the Scot to step in with effective right handers. It was not until the fourth round, however, that Watt really opened up. Midway through the session he caught Martins with a series of blows to the head that sent the Ghana boxer staggering back against the ropes. Watt followed up his advantage by connecting with a perfectly timed left hook to the jaw which dropped Martins to the canvas where he took the full count while resting on one knee.

Boxing News
30 October 1968

Jim Watt's left hook from a southpaw stance is sparingly but judiciously used and it is going to be a big factor in his future. More than any other punch, it won him his first professional fight and also his second at Hamilton Town Hall against Irishman Alex Gibson of Belfast. He really only showed it after two minutes of the second round and Gibson, in a real slow-motion fold-up, crumpled to the boards. The Irishman managed to drag himself up just before the ten-second count was completed, but he was out on his feet and the referee was correct in not allowing another punch to land. Watt was quietly impressive, workmanlike but not flashy, and it will not be long before he is stepped up to tougher opposition.

David Stewart
Evening Citizen
11 December 1968

Jim Watt, of Glasgow, outclassed and outpunched Victor Paul, of Nigeria, on his way to an eight-round points victory at

Govan Town Hall last night. Watt did not lose a round in a non-stop battle. The twenty-year-old ex-British amateur lightweight champion scored a maximum 40 points with $38\frac{1}{2}$ to 'iron man' Paul who boasts, 'No one can put me down.' Watt, having only his third professional fight, confirmed his rating as Scotland's best young prospect as he ruthlessly exploded barrages of punches against Paul's chin. How the Nigerian, rated No. 4 in the Empire, survived some of the bruising attacks is a mystery. In the last two rounds Paul survived on courage alone.

James Sanderson
Scottish Daily Express
10 April 1969

Having only his fourth pro fight and his first outside Scotland, Jim 'Baby Face' Watt, Glasgow ($9-8\frac{1}{2}$), beat experienced Jamaican Winston Thomas, Northolt ($9-9\frac{1}{2}$) in one minute of the eighth and final round at London's World Sporting Club. A fierce left hook to the chin, following a correct southpaw right jab, hurled Thomas between the two bottom ropes and the count had reached eight before he got up. Then a volley of hooks to the head had Thomas in dire trouble in a neutral corner as referee Benny Caplan raced across the ring to stop the fight. Watt was always on top. He is a good mover and, at this stage of his development, bears comparison with another southpaw, the great Dave Charnley. His trouble now is going to be finding opposition.

Boxing News
15 September 1969

Jim Watt, Glasgow ($9-10$), outpointed tough Tommy Tiger, Leicester ($9-13\frac{1}{2}$) at the National Sporting Club by the comfortable margin of $40-38\frac{1}{2}$ points over eight rounds. The southpaw Scot kept his educated right jab on target in every round and avoided most of the right counters the ever-willing Tiger was ready to throw. Only in the last two rounds did Watt start to put combination punches together and a smart right to the chin from the Leicester lad gave him due warning not to be too adventurous. This was Tiger's 111th and final fight.

Boxing News
24 November 1969

Victor Paul, Nigeria (9.11¼), was very lucky to beat Jim Watt, Glasgow (9.10¾) at the NSC. Just before the end of the sixth round a clash of heads opened a cut over the Scot's right eye and referee Sid Nathan stopped the fight in Paul's favour after a long and careful inspection. Watt was a long way ahead on points at the unfortunate ending, scoring easily with strong southpaw jabs. But the Scot needs to show more variety and aggression if he is to get among the real money, while Paul looks as though he has had too many hard fights.

Boxing News
16 February 1970

Jim Watt, the Glasgow lightweight, survived a bad cut near his left eye in the first round and stopped Victor Paul, Nigeria, in the fifth at the National Sporting Club. It was the third meeting between the two, with the score standing at one all. When Watt went back to his corner at the end of the first round with blood streaming from his left eyebrow it seemed that Paul was all set to take the lead in the series. But Watt reacted by taking complete charge of the fight. He boxed so well that Paul scarcely landed another punch. The Scot punched so positively that the Nigerian was in trouble as soon as the second round started. Paul was dropped for a count of two midway through the round and was down again just before the bell. He was twice wrestled to the floor as he held on to Watt, trying not to take any more punches. Finally, referee Harry Gibbs stopped the contest to save Paul from unnecessary punishment.

Scotsman
1 June 1970

Glasgow's Jim Watt (9–9), the former ABA champion, stopped

Welsh lightweight champion Bryn Lewis, of Porthcawl (9–7½), at the end of the sixth round. The clever Scot started slowly but soon showed a style highly appreciated by the Great International Sporting Club audience. His accurate punching had Lewis continually trapped against the ropes and powerless to counterattacks. After a one-sided sixth round that Lewis was lucky to survive the referee rightly called a halt. Watt's clear-cut win was a fine result for the Scot who produced some of the best boxing seen at this Nottingham club all season.

Boxing News
15 June 1970

Scottish southpaw lightweight Jim Watt will, in the opinion of manager James Murray, be ready for champion Ken Buchanan in the next year. Watt, ex-ABA champion, has won seven of eight professional bouts. He has craft and can punch, but accepts the need for experience before taking such a formidable step-up in class as Buchanan. 'Buchanan is a capable man and must never be underestimated,' said Murray. 'You have to be able to hit hard and often to beat him.' Watt was twenty-two on July 18. He has outclassed most of his opponents and his sole loss was due to an eye injury. In action, Watt is cool and calculating. He usually looks best against opponents who take the fight to him. Critics accuse him of showing too much caution but manager Murray says: 'Jim plans each fight. You can never afford to take chances in the professional ring. Maybe Jim appears a bit careful but you will never see him hanging his chin out. . . .' Murray has supreme confidence in Watt's capabilities and rates the day Watt walked into the Cardowan Amateur Club as 'the luckiest day in my life'. Watt doesn't particularly like watching boxing and says he is in the game for the good things he can get out of it. 'Being perfectly honest about it,' he says, 'I want material rewards. A nice house, a nice car and things like that. The money, after all, is why I turned professional.'

Graham Houston
Boxing News
August 1970

Some come smooth and some come spiteful. Glasgow light-weight, Jimmy Watt, only came with what he needed . . . a Warnock-style southpaw right hook to the solar plexus. It was a savage, crippling punch that dismantled an unsuspecting Sammy Lockhart and left a disbelieving Ulster Hall ringside clamouring for more. Question is: Who can they get to fight the hammering-hitting Scot? Lockhart was knocked out in the second round, pole-axed by one punch, that wicked right. It travelled further than good body punches usually do but its effect was instantaneous. For a moment, Lockhart looked as if he had been run through with a sword. He doubled in two, grimacing in pain, legs turned to rubber, and sank to the canvas, his bottom cushioned on the ropes. . . . It was the most impressive win of the year by a visiting fighter to Ulster.

Jack Magowan
29 October 1970

The run of successes enjoyed by Ron Clifford, Pudsey (9–11¾), ended when an injured right hand compelled him to retire midway through the fourth of his scheduled eight rounder with former ABA champion Jim Watt, Glasgow (9–10¾), at Leeds. It is only fair to say that Clifford, with a growing reputation, appeared to be lagging behind the fast and clever Scottish southpaw. Clifford sustained a cut over his right eye in the first round but good cornerwork checked it. But as the contest proceeded the versatility of Watt looked likely to prove decisive.

Boxing News
1 December 1970

Scottish lightweight stylist Jim Watt (9–11¾), comfortably outpointed David Presenti, of Lyons (9–8¾), a leading conten-der for the French title, in an eight-round bout at the Albany Hotel, Nottingham. It was Watt's tenth success in his eleven paid fights to date and he was never really extended although the smaller Frenchman always looked something of a busy character. His courage was applauded by the members of the

Great International Sporting Club, but it was obvious from the outset that his disadvantage in both height and reach would prove an insurmountable obstacle. Presenti was deputizing for his stablemate Leonard Dessi and never really fathomed the Scot's southpaw stance. Watt was able to pick his punches and several times jolted back the Frenchman's head with snappy straight lefts to the head. Presenti's face bore signs of a battle in the later stages, but he continued to show his pluck although he was well outpointed in the end with Watt collecting $39\frac{3}{4}$ points to his 39.

Boxing News
11 January 1971

Jim Watt, the No. 1 challenger for the British lighweight title, was an impressive winner over Henri Nesi (France) at the National Sporting Club. Halfway through the sixth round of a ten-round bout referee Harry Gibbs stopped the fight to save the Frenchman from unnecessary punishment. The Scot was on top from the start. For two rounds he allowed the Frenchman to make the running and scored well with sharp counters. But from the start of the third until the end of the fight Watt dominated completely. He hit Nesi with right jabs, following lefts and fierce right hooks to the body almost without reply. The Frenchman, hands held high, did his best to keep out of real danger but his few counterpunches were always picked off by Watt who continued to land punches almost as and where he wished. The fight was halfway through the sixth round when Nesi, pinned on the ropes, took a succession of jabs and hooks and the referee stopped the fight.

Scotsman
22 March 1971

Jim Watt, Glasgow's twenty-three-year-old southpaw, last night won the right to fight Ken Buchanan for the British lightweight title. He stopped fellow Scot Willie Reilly after one minute thirty-five seconds of the seventh round at the Empire Pool, Wembley. Blond Watt won the fight when a gash

opened over Reilly's right eye and referee Harry Gibbs
decided he could box no more. The crowd booed this untimely
ending for at this stage Watt was only slightly ahead on points
and Reilly fans saw every chance of their hero winning this
final eliminator. But to me it looked as if Watt was going to
edge this fight anyway. His leads had been biting into Reilly's
face from the opening bell and just before the end he was
switching to left crosses that pounded Reilly's head. Reilly
gamely tried to slip the leads and come in with bursts of
counterpunching, but was reprimanded for low punches.
Then, as Watt tried to take complete control, the cut opened
and ended all Reilly's hopes. Watt still seems a long way from
presenting a formidable challenge to world lightweight king
Buchanan.

Sydney Hulls
Daily Express
27 September 1971

Glasgow's Jim Watt became a royal and gory hero last night
in London's Café Royal. For the twenty-three-year-old came
back from what looked like a certain defeat to stop ex-French
champion Leonard Tavarez in the ninth round of a scheduled
ten-rounder. Watt was covered in blood and covered in glory.
Watched by Prince Philip in this charity show staged by the
National Sporting Club, Watt passed his toughest test as a
professional. And he did it by producing a barrage of power
punching in rounds six, seven and eight to wipe out the major
drawback of a cut eye in round two. The cut worsened as the
fight progressed and London referee Harry Gibbs inspected
the wound twice between rounds before allowing the Scot to
continue. Tavarez, who twice took world lightweight champion Ken Buchanan the distance, proved a handful for the
notoriously slow starter Watt. By the halfway stage he looked
in trouble against the Frenchman – behind on points and with
his eyebrow injury looking bad. But then he staged his glory
comeback, catching Tavarez with stunning short left and right
hooks. In the ninth, Watt was hitting his opponent at will and

when he released a barrage of punishing punches to the head, referee Gibbs rushed in to stop it.

Dick Currie
Daily Record
November 1971

Jim Watt, twenty-three-year-old Glasgow fighter, will become lightweight champion of Britain in succession to Ken Buchanan at Nottingham on February 1. The blond, outwardly placid young man, who likes to sit alone strumming his guitar and singing Negro blues songs, meets fellow-Scot Willie Reilly for the title relinquished by Buchanan who says: 'I first saw Jim Watt four years ago. I thought then that he was as fine a prospect as I have ever seen. He could do a very great deal for Scotland and the day could come when we might meet. I wish him well. He has the talent to give Scotland a very big boost.

James Sanderson
Scottish Daily Express
21 December 1971

Willie Reilly, twenty-four-year-old Wembley-Scot, won the vacant British lightweight title by stopping Glasgow's Jim Watt on injury in the tenth round at Nottingham Ice Rink. Reilly thus succeeds Ken Buchanan, the world titleholder, as British champion. But it was a hollow victory. Blond southpaw Watt looked to be getting on top when his right eyebrow was gashed, forcing referee Roland Dakin to stop the fight. Reilly ($9-6\frac{1}{2}$) boxed cleverly in the early stages but it looked as if Watt ($9-6\frac{1}{4}$) would catch up eventually. Reilly is now committed to defend against Tony Riley from Coventry but twenty-three-year-old Watt deserves an immediate crack at the winner. Watt has now been stopped twice on cut eyes in fifteen professional fights. He is championship material but tender brows look like being his downfall. A head clash ripped open a wicked gash over Watt's right eye in the last seconds of the seventh round. Watt chased Reilly all around the ring in rounds eight and nine, but the Anglo-Scot started a comeback

in the tenth and referee Dakin finally called a halt after a left
hook caught Watt on the injured eye.

Boxing News
1 February 1972

Jim Watt, the twenty-three-year-old Glasgow lightweight who
failed in his bid to win the British title in February, gets an
unexpected chance to win the crown at the Midland Sporting
Club, Solihull, tomorrow night. The man who beat Watt for
the title, Anglo-Scot Willie Reilly, sensationally quit boxing
last week and Jim and Tony Riley (Coventry) have now been
matched for the vacant championship. Despite his short-
notice recall to the big time – Reilly should have been defending it against Riley tomorrow – big-punching Watt is so
confident of victory that he has refused a 50–50 split of the
purse money. Says manager Jim Murray: 'We mean to win
this one. In fact, we're looking for a victory inside the distance. We have asked that the cash be split 60–40. That's how
much we fancy our chances.

Tommy Workman
Evening Citizen
2 May 1972

Jim Watt is back home in Glasgow as British lightweight
champion and ready to take on all comers. At the Midland
Sporting Club, Solihull, last night Jim became the third Scot
in succession to hold this title after stopping Tony Riley
(Coventry) in the twelfth round. Later Jim, who had stepped
in at just more than a week's notice to replace retired champion Willie Reilly, said he would not put the title in cold
storage. Before the contest Jim told me he wanted to win the
crown and defend it twice as quickly as possible to clinch a
Lonsdale Belt. This is now his main objective. Southpaw Watt
started impressively, built up the points and then, with Riley
showing two cuts around the eyes, the Glasgow man stepped
up the pressure with solid hooks to the head and body. When
referee Harry Gibbs intervened with four seconds of the

144

twelfth round remaining it came as no surprise and the Riley camp had no complaints. Who knows, in time we could have Watt meeting Ken Buchanan for the world lightweight title.

John Quinn
Evening Times
3 May 1972

Jim Watt, twenty-four-year-old British lightweight champion from Glasgow, won an inside-the-distance decision at the National Sporting Club in London last night. And then, minutes after the end of the fight, he was publicly slammed by former world champion Ken Buchanan. 'It is the first time I have ever seen him in action and he is even worse than I thought,' said Buchanan, who challenges Watt for the British title in Glasgow on 29 January. Southpaw Watt had stopped Noel McIvor from Luton with a cut eye in the third of an eight-round contest – a warm-up for his British title defence. And spying from the front row was Buchanan. His verdict: 'If he fights like that against me, then it won't last long.' Certainly Watt was not at his best. It was his first fight since winning the title and he showed some ring rust. But when the dramatic end came, he looked well in control.

Dick Currie
Daily Record
11 December 1972

He talks like Humphrey Bogart – I just hope he can come out fighting like him. That's Jim Murray, manager of British lightweight champion Jim Watt, talking about his man's next opponent, Ken Buchanan. The twenty-seven-year-old former champion of the world challenges twenty-four-year-old Watt for his British title at the new Albany Hotel in Glasgow on Monday night. If you get the feeling that Murray doesn't like Buchanan and that he is trying to needle him, then you're right on both counts. Murray is determined to turn the title contest into one of the great grudge fights. Not as a sales gimmick either, for the 500 seats in the Albany's St Andrew's suite have been sold out for months now. It is because he believes that a toe-to-toe battle would be made to measure for Watt, an acknowledged heavy hitter. 'Buchanan has said a lot of uncomplimentary things about Jim and myself,' says Murray. 'He called me the worst manager in Britain and marked Jim down as a two-round job who shouldn't be allowed in the same ring as him. Well I hope he is ready to back his hard words with harder deeds. I want this to be a fight where one or the other will be carried out of the ring. I know it won't be Jim Watt. Buchanan is a light puncher and it makes me laugh when I hear him say he'll annihilate Jim. I have gone over his record with a magnifying glass and have come to the conclusion that he couldn't annihilate a mouse. . . .'

Tommy Workman
Evening Citizen
January 1973

With a face that was a mass of lumps, nicks and bruises, Ken Buchanan let it be known that he may well relinquish his newly won British title for a second time. 'I will be giving it serious consideration during the next few weeks,' he told me. 'I have a contract for a return world title fight with Roberto Duran in New York around June, when I might be expected to be called on to defend the British championship. I consider that Jim Watt is a great fighter for whom I have not one nasty word, despite what his manager Jim Murray, who afterwards refused my hand, says about me. With seventeen contests compared to the forty-seven I have had, he is a boy in the matter of experience, but he did a man's job. He deserves another championship chance and I certainly don't want another one with him like tonight.' So splendidly did Watt fight that many considered Buchanan had been considerably flattered by Edinburgh referee George Smith in being adjudged the winner by $74\frac{1}{4}$ points to $72\frac{1}{2}$ points. And there were those who considered that Watt had done sufficient to hold on to his title. I should not quarrel with Mr Smith's arithmetic, although the appointing of an official from Bucha-

146

nan's native city of Edinburgh was puzzling and surely unwise.

Walter Bartleman
London Evening Standard
29 January 1973

Former British lightweight champion Jim Watt (9–10½), who lost his title to former world champion Ken Buchanan in January, gained a comfortable points win in an entertaining eight-rounder with fellow-Scot Johnny Cheshire (9–12¾) at the Midlands Sporting Club, Solihull. Referee Frank Parkes scored it 39½–38¾ in Watt's favour. Eager for a return with Buchanan, Watt used his southpaw right jab and swift counterpunching to pile up the points in the early rounds. Cheshire kept busy and went for the body, but he was warned twice for hitting low and slapping. He tossed several good right handers and had a measure of success in the sixth and seventh rounds, but Watt's nimble footwork kept him out of trouble. Cheshire put up a good performance and was always ready to have a go, but Watt was simply too smart for him.

Boxing News
9 May 1973

Lightweight Jim Watt, of Glasgow, took a step towards regaining his British title last night at Govan Town Hall. He did so by stopping Noel McIvor, the Southern Area champion from Luton, in the fourth round of their scheduled eight-round contest with a cut eye. Watt had his opponent bleeding as early as the second round and by concentrating on the wound made sure it was just a matter of time before he gained the decision. Afterwards Watt's manager Jim Murray, who promoted the show and proved there is still a market for professional boxing in Scotland, said: 'Jim had to win this one to earn a crack at the British title he lost to Ken Buchanan.'

Ian Broadley
Daily Record
7 June 1973

Jim Watt, of Glasgow, last night confirmed his ranking as No.
1 contender for Ken Buchanan's British lightweight title when
he outpointed fellow Glaswegian Angus McMillan over eight
rounds at Govan Town Hall. Ex-British champion Watt, who
lost his crown to Buchanan, had the fright of his life when he
was knocked down for a count of three in the first round by a
McMillan right hook. But southpaw Watt, who fought with a
swelling under his left eye for virtually the whole of the fight,
recovered to win well. Brave McMillan, cut on the forehead
and bleeding heavily from the nose, put up a good show. He
had six brothers, all of them boxers, at the ringside to cheer on
his vain attempt to get a crack at Buchanan. The referee gave
Watt 79½ points to McMillan's 78½.

James Sanderson
Daily Express
5 October 1973

Jim Watt, blond Scottish southpaw lightweight, gained an
important upset victory when he stopped South African
champion Andries Steyn on a cut eye in the seventh of their
scheduled ten-rounder in Johannesburg. Watt, former British
champion, boxed cleverly and punched solidly after a cautious
first round. He seemed to be in front on points at the finish.
The Scot grew in confidence when a deep cut was opened over
Steyn's right eye in the third round after what looked like a
clash of heads. Steyn, fighting to preserve his high world
rating, fought desperately in the fourth to try and finish the
fight. But Watt repeatedly picked him off with stabbing right
jabs and Steyn's eye was now bleeding freely. Steyn landed
some good left hooks in the fifth, but Watt remained cool. The
Scot kept plugging away with right jabs in the sixth to keep
Steyn contained and the fight was stopped after one minute of
the seventh following an inspection of the South African's
worsening eye injury by a ringside doctor.

Boxing News
16 February 1974

THE JIM WATT SCRAPBOOK 1964-80

Jim Watt outpointed Kokkie Olivier over ten rounds in Johannesburg. Watt gave one of the finest exhibitions of boxing seen in South Africa for many years. The pale-faced Scot must on the evidence of this performance climb most deservedly into the world lightweight ratings. During and at the end of the contest both Watt and Olivier received loud and long applause for their skill, speed and stamina. Watt gave a delightful performance of jabbing and counterpunching. His stinging right seldom wavered from its target – which was Olivier's head. Going into the last two rounds, Watt held a lead of two points on most scorecards which meant Olivier had to pull out almost supernatural strength and stamina to share the decision. Olivier did just that in the ninth round, but the effort sapped his strength and the Scottish southpaw clinched a marvellous victory with his accurate and authoritative work in the final round.

Agency report
2 March 1974

Jim Watt, the Glasgow southpaw, again proved conclusively last night that he is the only lightweight in Britain capable of tackling British and European champion Ken Buchanan. At Caerphilly's Anglo-Welsh Sporting Club, Watt proved too strong for another top contender, Billy Waith of Cardiff, in a final eliminator for Buchanan's title, outpointing him over twelve rounds. Referee Sid Nathan scored it 119 points to Watt with 116½ to the Welsh lad. Watt was always in command in a rather slow-moving contest in which both men showed too much respect for each other. It was not until the fifth round, when Waith was cut, that Watt really took over, but even then he could not press home his advantage sufficiently to stop the Welshman. This is Watt's sixth consecutive win since losing his British title to Buchanan on points in Glasgow seventeen months ago. Since then, however, Ken has gone on to beat Antonio Puddu, of Italy, for the European title and is bidding for a world title bout. This could mean that Watt may face a long delay in meeting Buchanan or Ken may decide, as he did before, to give up his British title.

John Quinn
Evening Times
19 June 1974

I had my introduction to this story already typed with Jim Watt the winner. Then came the judges' decision in Tony 'Blue Jaguar' Morodi's favour and it was a short circuit that shocked me mightily. It proved to me once again that our judges give more points for aggression than skill. They must have been blindfolded to have missed Watt's clever counter-punching and superb ring generalship. The Scot was real mean on Morodi and in my book he didn't concede the South African more than four rounds in the ten. Watt is a master counterpuncher and avoids punches when standing his ground like a Highland sword dancer. It is decisions like this that will further outlaw us in the eyes of the boxing world.

Norman Canale
Johannesburg Sunday Times
26 October 1974

Jim Watt will win the British lightweight title in Glasgow's Albany Hotel tonight. This is my firm forecast when the former champion from Glasgow clashes with Anglo-Scot Johnny Cheshire for the vacant crown, which Ken Buchanan relinquished. The fight tops the St Andrew's Sporting Club bill and is scheduled for fifteen rounds. It's win or bust for twenty-six-year-old Watt, who has had only twenty-five professional fights in under seven years. Watt lost his title to Ken Buchanan in an epic fight at the Albany two years ago. Cheshire, who has lost ten of thirty-one paid fights, has looked good in sparring with another former champion, Jimmy Revie, but I still take Watt to win.

Dick Currie
Daily Record
27 January 1975

Jim Watt, a twenty-six-year-old electrician from Possilpark, Glasgow, last night regained the British lightweight title when he stopped his fellow-Scot Johnny Cheshire after two minutes fifty-five seconds of the seventh round at the St Andrew's Sporting Club. It was the end of a two-year wait for Watt and the realization of a burning ambition as he was once again acclaimed champion of Britain. He threw his hands high in the air as the referee, Wally Thom, stepped between him and the unfortunate Cheshire. With Ken Buchanan watching as the club's guest of honour, both fighters were piped into the ring and that was the end of the music as far as Cheshire was concerned. The Ayrshire-born man, now based in London, was, as all of us had feared, hopelessly out of his class.

Jim Reynolds
Glasgow Herald
27 January 1975

It was all so easy for British lightweight champion Jim Watt as he cantered to a points win over Cardiff substitute Billy Waith in their non-title ten-rounder at the Anglo-American Sporting Club in Mayfair's Hilton Hotel. Watt, twenty-six-year-old Glasgow southpaw, is due to meet Nigerian Jonathan Dele for the vacant Commonwealth title in Lagos in May and Waith provided him with an ideal warm-up. Referee Benny Caplan scored Watt the winner by $99\frac{1}{2}$–$95\frac{1}{2}$, or nine rounds to one. Waith's manager, Mac Williams, thought this was distinctly ungenerous to his fighter, yet there was no doubt in my mind that Watt had won comfortably enough. It was Watt's second win over Waith whom he outpointed at Caerphilly last June in a British title eliminator. Watt made his characteristic slow start, but took control of the fight from the fourth round. He had trouble getting his punches on target against a slippery and evasive opponent, but usually looked dominant against an opponent whose counters were too infrequent to be really effective.

Graham Houston
Boxing News
19 March 1975

British lightweight champion Jim Watt, from Glasgow, failed in his bid to win the Commonwealth boxing title here in Lagos today. He was outpointed over fifteen rounds by Spanish-based Nigerian Jonathan Dele, but the result was a lot closer than the referee Howard Jones's amazing scorecard indicated. For Jones made an unbelievable nine rounds even, gave five to Dele and just one to Watt. Most neutral onlookers – and there weren't many among the cheering, chanting Nigerian crowd – felt the Scot had boxed a clever fight on the defensive. Obviously, however, the referee was more impressed by Dele's non-stop aggression. He dominated the first three rounds and had Watt down for a count of eight in the second.* After that, though, Watt settled and Dele didn't land another really damaging punch.

Agency report
3 May 1975

Jim Murray, manager of British lightweight champion Jim Watt, has written to the European Boxing Union protesting about the decision that cost his fighter his European title chance. According to Murray, the split verdict that gave Frenchman André Holyk a twelve-round points victory over Watt in their eliminator at Lyons was 'a disgrace'. Murray said: 'There is no way that the judges could have genuinely arrived at this decision. Jim was a long way ahead and even if he lost the last two rounds he must have been the winner. I have written complaining about the verdict of the Italian and Belgian judges who gave Holyk their backing. The German judge told me that in his view Watt won by nine rounds to three.' Murray has also written to Ray Clarke, British Boxing Board of Control secretary, urging him to ask for a straight fight between Watt and the eventual winner of the European title which has been vacated by Ken Buchanan.

Ian Paul
Glasgow Herald
31 October 1975

* Jim Watt comments: 'I was down once during the fight and that was when we got in a tangle and both of us fell over. There was no count.'

Jim Watt, British lightweight champion, has joined the Terry Lawless stable. Contracts were signed this week. Watt will continue to live in Glasgow but will be making frequent trips to London. He will come down at weekends and for longer periods before fights. Manager Lawless emphasized that Watt continues to have the highest respect for his previous manager, Jim Murray. Terry feels he can give Watt a wider variety of sparring at his Canning Town gym. 'He'll be able to move around with Ray Cattouse and help Ray and can also work with John H. Stracey. Jim gave John a hiding when they met in the ABAs when John was a kid, but that'll be a joke between them when they meet socially for the first time.' Lawless intends to feature Watt as much as possible on the London commercial shows, both at major and small hall promotions. 'He'll have a lot of fights to build up a bit of a following,' said Lawless.

Boxing News
February 1976

Jim Watt of Glasgow made an Ali-like announcement after stopping George Turpin (Liverpool) in four rounds at the Royal Albert Hall, London, last night. As he rubbed himself down in the dressing-room afterwards he said: 'I'm not boasting but I think I'm the best lightweight in Europe.' His new manager Terry Lawless, who has world champion John Stracey in his stable, nodded his agreement. 'I'm pleased that Jim has got that fight out of the way,' said Lawless. 'He will be back in London in a fortnight to help Stracey prepare for his world title defence and to get himself ready to meet Jim Revie at the Cunard Hotel on 30 March.' It was Watt's high-voltage short right to the jaw that started Turpin on the road to his first defeat in ten bouts as a professional. The Glasgow boy, who holds the British title, bounced the Liverpool lad up and down for counts of nine, eight, nine and nine before referee Sid Nathan intervened. It was a merciful end.

Scotsman
2 March 1976

British lightweight champion Jim Watt (Glasgow) presented a new image last night in London's Cunard Hotel where he was boxing Anglo-Scot Jimmy Revie. The dinner-jacket set enjoyed the spectacle. Watt in the past has shown a large measure of caution in his approach, carefully pacing himself and inclined at times to be a wee bit pedestrian in his efforts. His new manager, Terry Lawless, has given him a more positive outlook and this was excitingly demonstrated by Watt's increased punch rate. He was at the throat of the former British featherweight champion almost before the note of the first bell had faded, and until the referee stopped the fight in round seven because of a cut over Revie's right eye, Watt was punching with speed, force and accuracy. Afterwards Watt said he was happy with his showing. So were the crowd. So was matchmaker Mickey Duff, who promises the new-look Watt a lot of work, with perhaps a world title shot at the end of his particular rainbow.

Bill Brown
Evening Times
30 March 1976

Jim Watt, British lightweight title-holder, turned in a true champion's performance when he belted game Hector Diaz (Dominican Republic) to defeat in four one-sided rounds at the Anglo-American Sporting Club, Mayfair. Referee Mike Jacob stepped between them after one minute twenty-five seconds of the fourth round with Diaz taking heavy punishment against the ropes. There was some booing but no complaints from Diaz's corner. In fact his manager had been trying to catch the referee's eye – presumably to tell him to stop the fight – for approximately half a minute before the end. Watt, twenty-seven-year-old Glasgow southpaw, looked good. He jabbed with authority, stabbing the right into Diaz's face time and time again and he scored frequently with well-placed left hooks. Diaz, to his credit, kept trundling forward but he was not in Watt's class and when Jim clicked into top gear in the third round Diaz was just left behind.

Simon Euan-Smith
Boxing News
10 May 1976

A blatant butt cost Glasgow's Jim Watt a third-round defeat in last night's Wembley fight against Johnny Claydon from West Ham. The Claydon head bobbed forward menacingly in the second round and Watt staggered back with blood streaming from a cut at the side of his right eye. Manager Terry Lawless worked frantically on the injury during the one-minute interval, but it was to no avail. Rough-house fighter Claydon re-opened the cut with almost the first punch of round three and, after twenty seconds, referee Roland Dakin signalled that the British champion could not carry on. Claydon had been left red-faced and blinking by the speed of Watt's punching, but all this changed once the London lad saw the blood flowing from the corner of Watt's eye. At the finish, Claydon's hysterical supporters raised a Wembley-sized cheer and some of them tried to invade the ring. Claydon could scarcely believe he had landed such an upset victory and he danced with his supporters all the way back to the dressing-room.

John Lloyd
Daily Express
22 June 1976

Jim Watt, British lightweight champion from Glasgow, impressed with the verve and crispness of his combination punches as he outclassed game Italian Franco Diana in every one of the six rounds their scheduled eight-rounder went at Wembley. Referee Paddy Sower showed excellent timing as he stepped in at two minutes fifty seconds of the sixth to save Diana who was way behind with no hope of winning. Southpaw Watt (9–10¾) went aggressively into chunky, crewcut Diana from the start. He jabbed snappily before whipping in right hooks and bringing up powerful left uppercuts to the body through the centre of Diana's defence. 'Clusters, Jim!' manager Terry Lawless kept calling out from the corner and Watt obliged from the second round, putting together some impressive sequences. It was a positive-minded showing from Watt who seems to have undergone something of a stylistic change under Lawless's guidance. He has turned into basically an attacking fighter and this was a real champion's performance.

Boxing News
12 October 1976

Jim Watt (Glasgow) retained the British lightweight title in front of his home crowd at the St Andrew's Sporting Club last night when he stopped Johnny Claydon after two minutes thirty-five seconds of the tenth round. The win gave Watt outright ownership of a Lonsdale Belt after eight years as a professional and also gave him sweet revenge for a defeat by the Londoner in June. Glasgow belonged to Watt last night. The fans were solidly behind him from the start and gave him a standing ovation at the end. Never in the four years of the club has a fighter received such acclaim – and it was deserved. Watt had Claydon down four times for counts of eight before the Birkenhead referee Wally Thom called a halt – and the end came none too soon for the Englishman who must have found the ring something of a torture pit.

Jim Reynolds
Glasgow Herald
21 February 1977

Jim Watt will be an angry boxer when he steps into the St Andrew's Sporting Club ring in Glasgow tonight, bidding to become Britain's third European champion. The Scots-born southpaw lightweight is angry because he's a boxer without a title . . . and he's out of pocket. Watt, twenty-nine, meets Frenchman André Holyk for the vacant lightweight crown just twenty-six days after reluctantly giving up his British title – a decision that cost him an estimated £6000. Last month, Watt was scheduled to earn £8000 for defending his British title against Londonderry challenger Charlie Nash. But he was forced to surrender his crown when the Irishman insisted on fighting in Northern Ireland. Watt believed the risk of trouble was too great. Now his purse for the European fight is a mere £2000 and manager Terry Lawless says: 'Jim was sick when he had to give up his title. He badly wants another.' Victory tonight will mean sweet revenge for Watt. He and Holyk, twenty-six, met in a European title eliminator in France in October 1975, with the Frenchman winning a disputed points decision. It is twenty-four years since Peter Keenan outpointed France's Maurice Sandeyron at Firhill to become the last Scotsman to win a European title in Glasgow. But Watt is an improved fighter since Lawless took him over and if he can survive the opening few rounds – he is a notoriously slow starter – I can see him stopping Holyk in about round eleven.

Ron Wills
Daily Mirror
5 August 1977

Jim Watt sensationally became the European lightweight champion in just one minute twenty-two seconds at the St Andrew's Sporting Club, Glasgow, last night. The twenty-nine-year-old Moodiesburn southpaw looked on in amazement as French champion André Holyk was led crying to his corner with blood gushing from a cut right eyebrow. The ending came so soon, everyone – including Watt – was shocked. For, really, there had been little time for action. It happened after the first serious clash. Watt landed a crushing left hook to the body then two right crosses near the Frenchman's right eye. Blood gushed from a cut and immediately Italian referee Amleto Bellagamba led Holyk to his corner. And after a doctor had inspected the wound, the fight was stopped so Watt was European champion – in record time. And, ironically, it was his old rival, Ken Buchanan, the former title holder, who presented him with the championship belt.

Dick Currie
Daily Record
5 August 1977

Scotland's Jim Watt kept his European lightweight crown last
night. But he found it much tougher in the Solihull defence
against Spaniard Jeronimo Lucas – stopped in ten – than in
Glasgow three months ago. Then he stopped Frenchman
André Holyk in just eighty-two seconds. This time Lucas was
a handful. He constantly caught the southpaw champion with
right crosses. But in the sixth Watt shook the thirty-year-old
Castilian with a left hook that left him grabbing the Scot
around the waist to save himself. The fight almost didn't take
place when Italian referee Angelo Poletti found the ring
seventeen inches short of the minimum sixteen feet. But the
managers agreed to go on. By the end of the seventh Lucas
had a nick over his left eye and in the eighth was in serious
trouble. The Spaniard's eye injury was opened up but the
referee, after a long look, decided to let Lucas continue. After
the ninth, Lucas went back to his corner shaking his head in
despair and in that fateful tenth the ref stepped in.

Colin Hart
Sun
16 November 1977

Jim Watt, the fighting Scot, and his European lightweight title
challenger, Perico Fernandez, snarled a spate of terrible
insults at each other here in Madrid today. Partly the verbal
volleys were for the benefit of the box office at the Madrid
Palace of Sport where Watt tomorrow night defends his title
against the twenty-five-year-old confessed playboy Fernandez. But behind the blarney was real psychological warfare. Watt later quietly told me: 'If this fight goes the full
fifteen rounds, it will be a miracle if I remain the champion on
points. I've got to stop him inside the distance.' I fear Watt
may be right and it is going to be quite a job to stop
Fernandez. Manager Terry Lawless states: 'I think the
Spaniards have made a terrible mistake. They're treating Jim
too lightly. They think Fernandez has only got to turn up to
take the title. Somebody's in for a shock!' Watt's final fight
words: 'Whatever Fernandez can do he must do quickly. I'm

expecting him to throw everything into the early rounds. Then he will find out what I'm made of. . . .'

Sydney Hulls
Daily Express
17 February 1978

Magnificent Jim Watt (Glasgow) performed a miracle here in Madrid tonight when he retained his European lightweight title by punching former world light-welterweight champion Perico Fernandez (Spain) to a standstill in the giant Sports Palace. Before the fight the Glasgow boxer said he would have to stop Fernandez to keep the title. He was worried about a hometown decision, but his performance over fifteen rounds was so devastating, so clinical that even long before the end the fiercely partisan crowd were applauding the brilliant Scot. Watt became a pale-faced executioner here tonight, forcing Fernandez into three compulsory counts before being given a unanimous decision. Yet what a fright for Watt in the very first round. Fernandez came out like a whirlwind throwing wild swings to the head. Near the end of the round he landed with a left hook and a right cross and down went the champion. He looked to his corner and got up at eight as the bell sounded. As he walked back to his corner immediately above me, he looked down, gave a wink and a grin and shouted: 'Don't worry, I'll be all right.' That was the understatement of the night. From then on Watt dictated the fight, pinning Fernandez into corners and cutting off all points of retreat or getouts for the challenger. Watt thrashed Fernandez who only yesterday had boasted that he would give Watt a hiding.

Jim Reynolds
Glasgow Herald
17 February 1978

European lightweight champion Jim Watt coasted to an easy eight-round points win over Welshman Billy Vivian at the National Sporting Club in London last night. The twenty-nine-year-old Scot from Moodiesburn was never in serious trouble and treated the fight as a tough sparring session. Vivian, twenty-seven, was a fast mover but backpedalled for most of the fight. Londoner Harry Gibbs, Britain's best referee, made Watt a clear winner at the finish with a 79–74 points decision. This indicated that Watt had won six rounds, drawn one and lost one. Personally, I can't think of the round that he lost. Watt's only mistake in the fight was in letting the Welshman off the hook with a minute of the second round to go. He expertly delivered a quick one-two with a right followed by a left hook that sent Vivian reeling to the canvas for an eight count. But Vivian, although badly dazed, got back on shaky legs and managed to last the round.

Dick Currie
Daily Record
12 June 1978

Jim Watt will see his wife and kids for the first time in a month after he fights in Glasgow on Wednesday. Watt, Europe's lightweight champion, has become Britain's loneliest fighter while forcing himself into the world ratings. He has not been with his family in ten out of the last thirty months. Watt, who defends against Spaniard Antonio Guinaldo on Wednesday, spends the crucial weeks of his training in London with manager Terry Lawless, who has guided him from the verge of retirement to the world No. 2. He resents missing his family and has worked out his bitterness on a series of hapless opponents. When he joined Lawless he was twenty-seven and had lost his last two fights. He felt he had gone as far as he could, but decided to give Lawless and London one last try. The result has been nine victories – seven inside the distance – and one cut-eye defeat to Johnny Claydon whom Watt stopped in a re-match. Now, at thirty, Watt is poised to take a world title shot, hopefully this winter.

Frankie Taylor
Sunday People
15 October 1978

Jim Watt, at thirty, gets better and better. The fighting Scot's performance last night, in defence of his European lightweight title, must rate with any in his ten-year record. After five rounds at Kelvin Hall, Glasgow, Antonio Guinaldo of Spain simply surrendered – and for me that makes him a good judge. He raised his right hand in the air, turned his back and shook his head. There was some booing but only from the bloodthirsty. French referee Raymond Baldeyrou shrugged his shoulders as if to say he had no control over the situation. The British Boxing Board's reaction was to withhold part of Guinaldo's purse, the ancillary rights including the television fee. Surrenders are not officially acceptable. Maybe what concerned them was that the Spaniard arrived in Scotland with his fiancée, but fighters nowadays often bring their womenfolk with them. Take Muhammad Ali for instance. I see no point in taking sanctions against Guinaldo. Hurt in the first round, knocked down in the second, persued and pounded for the rest of it, there was nothing left for him except the considerable prospect of being badly damaged.

> Peter Moss
> *Daily Mail*
> 18 October 1978

European lightweight champion Jim Watt will meet Colombian Alfredo Pitalua for the vacant world title in his hometown of Glasgow. That was the exciting news from Glasgow's Lord Provost David Hodge yesterday after a lengthy get-together of the City's top officials with Watt, his manager Terry Lawless and promoter Mickey Duff. Although London has at least three indoor centres that could comfortably house the fight, Glasgow has no such venue. But contingency plans have been put into operation and the Kelvin Hall is to be filled with temporary seating. And 10,000 fans will be accommodated for the first world contest in Scotland since flyweight Jackie Paterson successfully defended his crown against Joe Curran of Liverpool in 1946. Finance for the seating will basically come from the Glasgow Sports Promotions Council. A burst of applause greeted the news that

Glasgow had won the big fight when Lord Provost Hodge made the announcement. Said the sports-minded No. 1 citizen: 'Glasgow belongs to Jim Watt and Jim Watt belongs to Glasgow. There have been problems in getting the fight for our city, but there was no way we would have lost this one.'

Jim Patterson
Daily Express
March 1979

Prize-fighting, having survived two centuries of controversy, raised itself to a new dignity in Glasgow, thanks to that decent family man Jim Watt. Boxing's latest ambassador could be passed any day in Sauchiehall Street as any common old working man. Yet by winning the world lightweight title by taming Alfredo Pitalua, a street fighter from Colombia, he put more pride back into Scottish sport than another compatriot, James Watt, put steam into his engine 200 years ago. Though the little black South American was almost devoid of defensive skill, Watt lived dangerously for twelve rounds. By keeping his cool and using an old-fashioned right-hand jab. the Scottish southpaw earned my award as Boxing Brain of Britain 1979. On my scorecard he was always in front. Even so he faced a crisis in the fifth round. It wasn't until he knocked Pitalua down that we were certain he would win the title. The world title with its £40,000-plus purse couldn't have happened to a nicer guy. His years of dedication and preparation in a gymn rather than a nightclub meant he didn't pick the pockets of the fans who paid £100,000 to cheer him. In all the years I have been watching boxing around the world I have never seen a more sporting performance by both competitors and customers.

Frank Butler
News of the World
17 April 1979

Jim Watt is an unassuming, unmarked boxing phenomenon who, in a few months, has become the Henry Cooper of

162

Scotland – and more! Lightweight champion of the world, he attracts the kind of hysterical adulation more associated with Muhammad Ali than with a quiet-spoken southpaw born thirty-one years ago in the rough Bridgeton area of Glasgow. That is why when he steps from his corner around 9.30 p.m. on Saturday evening to defend his crown against the power-punching Mexican Roberto Vasquez, Glasgow's Kelvin Hall will be a seething cockpit of emotion and noise. Not only is the Scottish idol being paid a British record purse of £75,000 but the warfare will be watched by a TV audience of between 150 and 200 million. Since he joined the Terry Lawless stable three and a half years ago, the slim, handsome Watt has become far more aggressive. And he will need it all against the menacing American-trained Vasquez. Twenty-one and only 5 ft 5 in tall, the counter-punching challenger erupted out of nowhere when, in Honolulu last July, he floored the original No. 1 contender, Hawaii's Andrew Ganigan, for seven and nine counts in the seventh round. The referee stopped the fight. What Vasquez has is a sleeping draught in either fist. Of his twenty wins in twenty-six bouts, eight have been by KO, nine on stoppages and three on points. He has lost four times and drawn twice. I once called Watt, 'the thinking man's boxer'. Today that description is even more true. Wily as an old fox with his unorthodox skills, he is not a dramatic performer. He just coldly destroys them. Backed by that blood-curdling Glasgow crowd, I am taking perfectionist Watt to outsmart and outpunch the big hitter from San Antonio.

Alan Hoby
Sunday Express
28 October 1979

March in the next challenger. World lightweight champion Jim Watt is ready to put up his 9 st 9 lb title again. Scot Watt, ninth-round destroyer of America's Roberto Vasquez in Glasgow, smiled yesterday: 'My hands aren't knocked up. Physically, I'm ready to go now with the next one. Mentally, well maybe I could do with a few weeks off. I was under so much pressure for this fight. When the bagpipes started playing me into the ring I felt the hairs coming up on the back of my neck and I thought to myself, "Oh no. These people want me to die for them again." I must admit that right now because of their support I feel that I'm unbeatable in Glasgow.' Saturday's affray was much like a bull fight, with the crowd roaring tartan 'Olés' every time a Scottish dart ripped into the unfortunate Vasquez's body. And it had the knockers decrying the American's right to challenge. My judgement is that Watt's flawless performance made the fight look over easy. Watt's right hand flickered in and out of the American's face with the speed and precision of a striking cobra. Eventually Californian referee Rudi Ortega had to step in after two minutes thirty seconds of the ninth round to save Vasquez from further punishment.

Sydney Hulls
Daily Express
3 November 1979

The feud between Jim Watt and Charlie Nash will finally be settled in Glasgow tomorrow night. Watt defends his world lightweight title against Irishman Nash to end the festering rift that has built up since the Scot's management decided that he should not risk fighting for the British 9 st 9 lb crown in Derry. That's where Nash, who won as an amateur in America, Russia, Spain and Denmark, has the support of wife, son and daughter, thirteen brothers and sisters and the regulars of the two pubs that he runs. Watt, thirty-one, relinquished the home title to go on and win the European championship and twenty-eight-year-old Nash later followed suit. Now Nash, with tongue-in-cheek bravado, fancies taking over Watt's precious World Boxing Council crown in the champ's backyard. The demands for Watt, articulate as a Gordonstoun don, to lay his educated fists on the Irishman were quickly heightened when Scotland watched live television coverage of Nash conquering fallen idol Ken Buchanan in Copenhagen. Buchanan, at thirty-four, was superb but make no mistake, Nash's points win was deserved. Watt, having honed himself in the heart of London's East End with the Lawless clan, thinks he will outstay Nash. 'Terry Lawless and I have watched his fight with Buchanan on video until I know him better than I know myself,' says the thorough champion. Watt is, I believe, a sure winner because I fancy he will punch too crisply, be able to change pace and pressure when required and retain the title without much argument from the three appointed officials.

Reg Gutteridge
London Evening News
13 March 1980

Wonderful Jim Watt knocked out Irish challenger Charlie Nash in the fourth round to retain the world lightweight championship at Kelvin Hall, Glasgow, last night. Brave Nash, the European champion, gave all he had but he hadn't the fire power to halt Glasgow's boxing idol. After Watt had been knocked down without a count in the first round, he annihilated Nash in a spasm of furious punching in the fourth. That knock-down didn't frighten Jim but it sent his wife Margaret scuttling in fear from the ringside. It was with a sigh that she heard the roar of the crowd acclaiming her husband still the champion near the end of the fourth round. Nash, sensing that Watt would need time to warm up, took the bout to the champion from the start, but just didn't have the armament to carry out his intentions. Watt took his best punches and when the Scot started to hit, Nash was in trouble and the end inevitable. Came the fourth and Watt relentlessly set about building up the barrage which left Nash twice struggling to beat the count and which finally saw the Derry man watch blearily as his title hopes slipped painfully away.

Pat Garrow
Scotsman
14 March 1980

The toughest judgements on really good fighters are delivered by their own pride. For Jim Watt, the status of champion could never be bestowed by the insertion of a few lines of print in the record books or the clasping of a fancy belt around his waist. It comes down to knowing he's the best and making sure everybody knows it. Watt won the World Boxing Council lightweight title in April 1979 and has defended it twice. But he says with quiet seriousness that when he goes in against the black American Howard Davis before close on 30,000 of his own people at Ibrox Park, Glasgow, he will feel more like a challenger than a champion. 'At least, I'll be as hungry as a challenger, as anxious to prove myself,' he said last week after showering off the sweat of perhaps the hardest training of his life. 'I've got the title and I know I'm the man, but a lot of people have been saying, "Yes, but there's that Howard Davis over in the States." This fight will just clear everyone's mind about it. This is the one that will establish me as the best in the world. I understand one Glasgow bookmaker has made Davis a shade of odds-on to beat me. That guy must be bloody crazy.'

Hugh McIlvanney
Observer
1 June 1980

Jim Watt is still king of the lighweights. The thirty-one-year-old Scot whipped American Howard Davis, twenty-four, at Ibrox Park, Glasgow, last night in front of 14,000 estatic fans. It was a brilliant exhibition by Watt. Controlled punching and tactical ring work brought him a unanimous points verdict after fifteen pulsating rounds. To me, he won nine rounds. And despite a cut under his left eye, sustained in the tenth, Watt was always too good, too experienced for the tall American. There was no doubt about the decision when the first outdoor fight in Scotland for twenty years finished with the boxers wrapped in each other's arms. Referee Carlos Padilla scored it 145–144. The South American judges, Guerra and Tovr, scored 149–142 and 147–144. After the verdict, Watt went to the microphone and led the crowd in a chorus of 'Flower of Scotland'. The smiling champion acknowledged the cheers, surrounded by friends and admirers. Watt proved to the world – via live TV satellite – that he is the undisputed lightweight kingpin. He out-thought and out-fought Davis, the first time the coloured New Yorker had been beaten in fourteen professional fights. It was, without question, Watt's best performance. He was never in trouble during one of the finest fights Scotland has ever seen.

Allan Herron
Sunday Mail
7 June 1980

Doubtless the Queen's Birthday Honours List due to be announced this week will contain the customary quota of sportsmen and sportswomen. In view of his achievements, the name of Jim Watt would not be out of place, although his latest success in retaining the world lightweight boxing title will have come too late to additionally influence his possible selection this time. That performance notwithstanding, Watt, with two previous successful defences behind him, has already done enough to gain the royal seal of approval. . . . Boxing, being the brutal, demanding arena that it is, has not always attracted individuals whose character can easily bear close scrutiny or be raised on a pedestal as an example to the youth of a nation. In an era of falling standards however, Jim Watt is refreshingly different. He is intelligent and articulate, confident but not cocksure, an obviously contented family man who delights in his wife and children. As important, perhaps, is the fact that he is unspoiled by his success. Surely a worthy candidate for some tangible royal recognition.

Leader article
Glasgow Herald
10 June 1980

Jim Watt, who only a week ago received the acclaim of Scotland when he successfully defended his world lightweight title, has received royal recognition in the Queen's Birthday Honours List. Watt, who is awarded the MBE, is among a number of sports personalities honoured, including Olympic ice-skating champion Robin Cousins, jockey Joe Mercer and England and Yorkshire cricketer Geoff Boycott.

Glasgow Herald
14 June 1980

Jim Watt, always under outside pressure before his four world lightweight title wins, knows he is walking an even more precarious tightrope for his defence in tomorrow's early hours. It will not be easy for him to push distracting thoughts to the back of his mind at Kelvin Hall, Glasgow, and get on with the job of beating American Sean O'Grady. The slim Scot, with the gift for doing and saying the right thing, feels his responsibility and knows British boxing is in need of a good night, one which emphasizes skill, competition and courage rather than the dangers, the ugliness of bad losers and the farce of mismatches. Until little more than a month ago we were enjoying the most successful age of the sport in this country. Then came the Johnny Owen tragedy, the Minter defeat and its crowd violence and the disappointing Mexicans at the Royal Albert Hall. Watt did as much as anyone to make the good times happen with his wins and the way he promoted himself. He has always had his country at heart too. . . . Watt has motivated himself this time by discovering that one more win would make him statistically the greatest boxer Scotland has every produced. Benny Lynch made three defences of the world flyweight title he won in 1935 before forfeiting it three years later by scaling nearly half a stone above the eight stone limit for a match with Jackie Jurich. If he can prove himself the best Scot, the only remaining target would be the five defences made by Welsh flyweight Jimmy Wilde between 1916 and 1923. First though there is O'Grady from Oklahoma. . . .

Peter Moss
Daily Mail
31 October 1980

Jim Watt proved yesterday that he is as callous as any fighting case that ever emerged from the Gorbals. Watt is a sweet-talking car salesman with a manner that would do credit to a bedside doctor but he tore apart the challenge of big-punching Sean O'Grady with cold, bloody disregard. Watt kept his world lightweight title by keeping his head throughout a chaotic pre-fight build-up and an electric Glasgow night in and out of the ring. It's a night I'll never forget. As Watt stormed back from the brink of defeat with his face a pattern of cuts and bruises, there was a deafening roar as O'Grady sustained a gaping gash across his forehead. Referee Raymond Balderou called on the ringside doctor to make a vital inspection of O'Grady's wound but the doctor was helping to tend a ringside reporter who had been taken violently ill as the fight reached its climax. The doctor, James N. Shea, coped magnificently with two jobs at once at a time when the fight could have ended in farce. Watt's twelfth round victory came after a clash of heads. It was not a deliberate butt but it was a definite case of canny Jim having his head in the right place at the right time. O'Grady's wound saved a battle Watt looked to be losing through injuries of his own on a night that saw Watt stretched to the limits of his determination, endurance and ringcraft.

Frankie Taylor
Sunday People
1 November 1980

Jim Watt's Professional Record

Born Glasgow, Scotland, 18 July 1948

1968

30 Oct.	Santos Martins Hamilton	W ko 4
11 Dec.	Alex Gibson Hamilton	W rsf 2

1969

10 Apl	Victor Paul Govan	W pts 8
15 Sept	Winston Thomas WSC, London	W rsf 8
24 Nov.	Tommy Tiger NSC, London	W pts 8

1970

16 Feb.	Victor Paul NSC, London	L rsf 6 (cut eye)
1 June	Victor Paul NSC, London	W rsf 5
15 June	Bryn Lewis GISC, Nottingham	W rsf 6
20 Oct.	Sammy Lockhart Belfast	W ko 2
1 Dec.	Ronnie Clifford Leeds	W ret 4

1971

11 Jan.	David Presenti GISC, Nottingham	W pts 8

22 Mar.	Henri Nesi	W rsf 6
	NSC, London	
27 Sept	Willie Reilly	W rsf 7
		(cut eye)
	(Final eliminator British lightweight title) Wembley	
1 Nov.	Leonard Tavarez	W rsf 9
	NSC, London	

1972

1 Feb	Willie Reilly	L rsf 10
		(cut eye)
	(Vacant British lightweight title) Nottingham Ice Rink	
3 May	Tony Riley	W rsf 12
	MSC, Solihull	
	(Vacant British lightweight title)	
11 Dec.	Noel McIvor	W rsf 3
	NSC, London	(cut eye)

1973

29 Jan	Ken Buchanan	L pts 15
	St ASC, Glasgow	
	(British title defence)	
9 May	Johnny Cheshire	W pts 8
	MSC, Solihull	
7 June	Noel McIvor	W rsf 4
	Govan	(cut eye)
5 Oct.	Angus McMillan	W pts 8
	Govan	

1974

16 Feb.	Andries Steyn	W rsf 7
	Johannesburg	(cut eye)
2 Mar.	Kokkie Olivier	W pts 10
	Johannesburg	
19 June	Billy Waith	W pts 12
	Caerphilly	
	(Final eliminator British lightweight title)	
26 Oct.	Anthony Morodi	L pts 10
	Johannesburg	

1975

27 Jan.	Johnny Cheshire St ASC, Glasgow (Vacant British title)	W rsf 7
19 Mar.	Billy Waith AASC, London	W pts 10
3 May	Jonathan Dele Lagos (Vacant Commonwealth lightweight title)	L pts 15
31 Oct.	André Holyk Lyons (Final eliminator European lightweight title)	L pts 12

1976 (Now managed by Terry Lawless)

2 Mar.	George Turpin Albert Hall, London	W ko 4
30 Mar.	Jimmy Revie Hammersmith	W rsf 7 (cut eye)
10 May	Hector Diaz AASC, London	W rsf 4
22 June	Johnny Claydon Wembley	L rsf 3 (cut eye)
12 Oct.	Franco Diana Wembley	W rsf 6

1977

21 Feb.	Johnny Claydon St ASC, Glasgow (British title defence)	W rsf 10
5 Aug.	André Holyk	W rsf 1 (cut forehead)
	(European lightweight title fight)	
16 Nov.	Jeronimo Lucas MSC, Solihull (European title defence)	W rsf 10 (cut eye)

1978

17 Feb.	Perico Fernandez Madrid (European title defence)	W pts 15
12 June	Billy Vivian NSC, London	W pts 8

| 18 Oct. | Antonio Guinaldo
Kelvin Hall, Glasgow
(European title defence) | W ret 5 |

1979

| 17 Apl | Alfredo Pitalua
Kelvin Hall, Glasgow
(Vacant WBC world lightweight title) | W rsf 12 |
| 3 Nov. | Roberto Vasquez
Kelvin Hall, Glasgow
(World title defence) | W rsf 9 |

1980

14 Mar.	Charlie Nash Kelvin Hall, Glasgow (World title defence)	W ko 4
7 June	Howard Davis Ibrox Park, Glasgow (World title defence)	W pts 15
1 Nov.	Sean O'Grady Kelvin Hall, Glasgow (World title defence)	W rsf 12 (cut forehead)